small group solutions for kids **13 SESSIONS**

13 VERY COOL STORIES

and Why Jesus Told Them

Standard®
PUBLISHING
Bringing The Word to Life

Cincinnati, Ohio

Published by Standard Publishing, Cincinnati, Ohio
www.standardpub.com

Content editor: Susan L. Lingo
Cover design: Scott Ryan
Interior design: Andrew Quach

ISBN 978-0-7847-2123-0

15 14 13 12 11 10 09 9 8 7 6 5 4 3 2 1

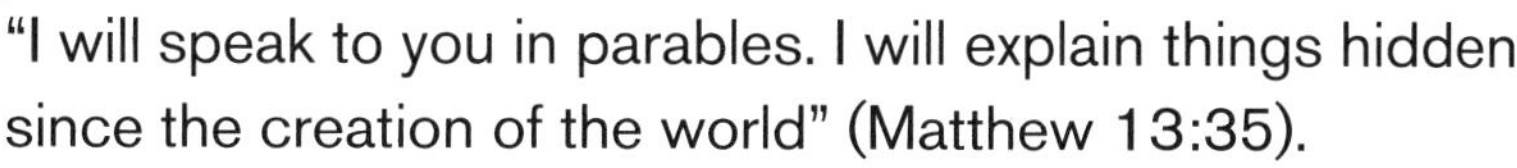

"I will speak to you in parables. I will explain things hidden since the creation of the world" (Matthew 13:35).

Contents

How to Use These Sessions

About These Sessions

First—thanks. Thanks for caring about children and helping your kids explore Jesus' parables. Though Jesus first shared his stories with adults, they're perfect for children too. Who's better than children at entering into stories?

So have fun, but know you'll be sharing powerful Bible truths as you move through these sessions. You'll help your children discover what Jesus had to say about the kingdom—and about living faithfully.

Welcome to Easy

These sessions make your life easy. They're light on supplies, quick to prepare, and long on fun. Because you don't have a lot of time each week to shop for supplies for crafts and object lessons, suggested supplies are common household items—things you probably already have in your kitchen, office, or garage. And because these sessions are created so beginning teachers or mature teenagers can be successful, no trained teachers are required! Because of the variety of options in each session, you can hold the attention of first graders through sixth graders. And even better, you'll help them discover truths about God!

Welcome to Simple Learning

Preparation is easy too. Each week you'll focus on one key point, one key Bible truth you want children to remember and apply in their daily lives. You'll drive home the point through Bible exploration, discussion, games, and activities that engage kids in multiple ways through multiple learning styles.

Welcome to Deep Bible Discovery

Each week your children will actually experience a Bible story in active, fun ways. Plus they'll discuss and apply what they learn. If that's what you're looking for—for your children to *do* God's Word instead of just hear it—you're in the right place. And you may wish to choose a kid-friendly Bible version to help your kids understand God's Word even more!

Welcome to Flexibility

Use these 45-minute sessions with kids wherever you find them. In Sunday school, during a second service, or while kids' parents are attending an adult class or small group. And if you're leading a house church, church plant, or using other building settings where Sunday school attendance is uncertain, these sessions are for you. They're . . .

- **Multi-aged**—suitable for mixed ages of elementary children
- **Easily adapted**—sessions work for 1 or 2 kids, 12 kids, or more
- **Relational**—children grow close to Jesus *and* each other
- **Stretchable**—brimming with options to fit varying time frames
- **Fun**—even easily distracted kids can engage, learn, and grow

Use These Sessions During Adult Small Groups

Not every parent looks forward to small group as a way to get out of the house and away from the kids. For many parents, leaving kids behind is precisely what they want to avoid.

"My kids are in school all day," says Sheila, a working mother of young children. "Why would I hire a babysitter so I can be away from them in the evening? For a church event that's supposed to make my family *stronger*? Besides, have you priced babysitters lately?"

13 Very Cool Stories and Why Jesus Told Them provides adult small groups with something fun, biblically solid, and purposeful for elementary-age kids to do while the adults are meeting. Some parents who do small groups instead of Sunday school may have children who don't attend Sunday school. This time would actually take the place of Sunday school for them. But even children who attend Sunday school will enjoy these active sessions. Here's how it works:

1. When the adult group begins, take children aside.

You'll need one adult or teenage leader to facilitate each Very Cool session. Ask adult small group members to take turns, or if you hire a babysitter anyway, consider paying a teenage volunteer leader from your children's ministry to lead the session. Have kids go to a different room than where adults meet. These sessions are fun—so they're sometimes loud!

2. Enjoy the session.

Relax! Each Very Cool session lasts about 45 minutes, with time-stretchers that easily fill another 15–30 minutes with on-target, Bible-point related activities. If the adult meeting goes long, you're ready!

3. Each week, the Howzitgoin' activity guarantees that you'll connect with kids.

It only takes a few minutes, but having children check in at the beginning of the session gives you valuable insights into what's happening in the lives of your kids. (Younger children will begin to open up after a few meetings and grow as they learn to express themselves and their feelings.)

4. Return children to their parents for prayer.

Most adult small groups and classes end with prayer. Consider bringing children back to their parents before the prayer time begins so kids can see their parents pray, watch other Christian adults turn to God, and hear how God answers prayers. Check with the adult group before bringing kids to join in!

Notice that parents get their "grown-up time" to meet with peers, yet they can still bring their kids to small group or class. And while parents are engaged in age-appropriate activities and study, so are the kids.

Even better: while the adults are forming closer relationships with each other and Jesus, so are the children!

Use These Sessions in Your Children's Ministry

All the same benefits already mentioned still apply—Very Cool sessions are easy to prepare, easy to teach, and connect with children in ways that make learning stick—which makes these 13 sessions perfect for a second service, a Sunday school class, or any other setting where leaders look to help children grow in their faith!

So dive in and discover how Jesus was able to wrap eternal truths in cool stories that still ring true, thousands of years after Jesus first shared them!

SESSION 1

The Story of the Good Shepherd

The Point: Trust Jesus.
Scripture Connect: John 10:11-15

Supplies for all Session 1 activities options: pencils, prepared poster, identical spoons (metal or plastic, at least 1 per child), Bible, 1 penny or nickel for each child (to keep), paper

The Basics for Leaders

Quick! When's the last time you saw a shepherd leading a flock of sheep around the countryside? Ever?

In Jesus' day, it was a common sight—so common that when Jesus painted a word picture of his relationship with his followers, he chose the image of a shepherd and sheep.

And not just any shepherd—Jesus claimed the role of a shepherd who owns the flock, who'll risk anything to protect his sheep . . . including his life.

That kind of commitment is rare. Think about who in your life is literally willing to die for you. For most of us, it's a short list.

As you share this story with your kids, you'll help them discover just how deep Jesus' love is for his followers—for us—and that we can trust Jesus too!

OPENING ACTIVITY—OPTION 1

HOWZITGOIN'

Time: about 5 minutes, depending on attendance
Supplies: pencils, prepared poster

Before kids arrive, draw a line on a poster. Place a 1 on the left end of the line, a 10 on the right, and a 5 in the middle. As kids arrive, ask them to pencil in their initials on the line.

Say: **If this past week was so awful you wish you'd slept through it, place your initials by the 1. If it was a great week you wish you could repeat, put your initials by the 10. Place your initials anywhere on the line that shows how you feel about this past week—except exactly on the 5. That's because there's no such thing as a week that's exactly half good and half bad!**

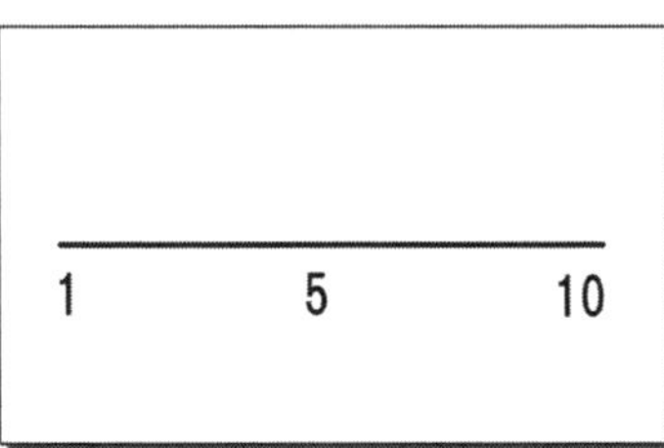

After kids have signed in, give them 30 seconds each to explain why they placed their initials where they did. Be sure to include your own initials and explain your placement on the line. Kids will begin to express themselves more over time—and hearing their stories will help you adapt this lesson to make it relevant to your kids' lives.

OPENING ACTIVITY—OPTION 2

A SPOON BY ANY OTHER NAME

Time: about 10 minutes
Supplies: identical spoons (metal or plastic, at least 1 per child)

Raid the kitchen! You'll want as many spoons as possible—but the spoons must be identical, all made in the same style. No metal spoons? A fistful of plastic spoons (or forks) will work.

Place the spoons in a pile on the floor. Say: **If I were a shepherd, I'd have one very big challenge: I can't tell the sheep apart. They all look the same, like these spoons look the same. But if you look closely, you'll find differences.**

Ask each child to take a spoon and study it. Challenge everyone to carefully examine his or her spoon for scratches, bumps, dents, or anything that makes the spoon distinctive. You can do the same with your spoon.

Next, ask children to name their spoons. Name yours Fluffy. Gather the spoons and mix them up. Toss them back on the floor with a rattle.

Say: **Our goal is to find our own spoons again. Let's start by calling them to see if they come to us.**

When that doesn't work say: **Guess these spoons are sort of like real sheep—they don't come when you call them. Oh well, go find your spoon!**

When children are certain they've located their unique spoons, have them circle up and discuss:

- ***You found your spoon among a bunch that looked pretty much the same. What helped you do that?***
- ***Jesus knows each of us—even though people all look pretty much the same. How do you think he does that?***
- ***How does it feel knowing that Jesus can pick you out of a crowd and knows your name?***

Say: **Today we'll explore a story Jesus told about being a shepherd . . . a good shepherd!**

Note: If kids can't find their own spoons, use this as an opportunity to point out that Jesus is a far better shepherd than we are. His love causes him to know each one of us perfectly.

Cool Story Game

Quick Change

Time: 5 minutes or more, as desired

Supplies: none

Ask children to each find a partner. If you have an odd number of children, jump in and be a partner.

Say: **Stand facing your partner and discuss this: If you could go anywhere on a vacation, where would you go—and why? What would you do there?**

Allow up to one minute for children to talk. Then say: **You've had a minute to get a good look at your partner. Now turn around or sit back-to-back so you can't see your partner.**

Silently change one thing about how you look. Something small, like unbuttoning a button, or changing your hair, or untying your shoe—anything to slightly change your appearance. Take 30 seconds.

After they make the changes, ask partners to turn around and look at each other. See how many pairs can identify what changed about their partners. Play several rounds. Then ask children to sit and discuss:

- ***What made this game easy or difficult?***
- ***What if I'd asked you to tell what your partner was thinking about? How well would you have done with that?***

Say: **Someone knows us well enough to tell when we change something about ourselves—and even what we're thinking. Today we'll dig into a story that has an important meaning: Jesus knows us!**

Cool BIBLE STORY

WOLF!

Time: 15 minutes
Supplies: Bible

Form your children into four groups: shepherds, hired hands, wolves, and sheep. Got just a few kids? You play the role of wolf and, if necessary, drop the sheep role. You're good to go with just two kids and yourself!

Say: **One day Jesus told a story that involved sheep and a shepherd. Jesus was trying to make a point to his listeners. These were Jewish leaders who said they were leading people closer to God . . . but they really weren't. Let's**

AGE-ALERT TIPS

Young children will especially enjoy impersonating sheep, so allow time for them to get in character and move around a bit before proceeding.

experience the story and see if we can discover a lesson for us.

Place the sheep in the center of the room on all fours. Ask them to get in character by delivering a few *baaaas*. Place your shepherds and hired hands near the sheep. Keep the wolf off to the side of the room.

Say: **I'm going to read aloud the story Jesus told his listeners. As I read, do what's described and what you think a wolf and sheep would do. Ready?**

Read John 10:11-15, pausing when there's action called for. Applaud your actors and ask kids to sit in a circle. Discuss the following questions:

- ***Two kinds of people were guarding the sheep: hired hands and shepherds. Why did they behave differently?***
- ***Jesus describes himself as one of those two kinds of guards. Which one? And why?***
- ***In what ways is Jesus a shepherd to us all? to you?***
- ***How do you feel knowing that Jesus is watching out for you?***
- ***In what ways does Jesus earn your trust?***

Say: **We don't have many people in our lives who'd die for us. But that's exactly what Jesus did . . . and he's alive again and watching out for us. That makes it easy to love him and trust him!**

AGE-ALERT TIPS

If you have mostly **older children** (4th, 5th, and 6th graders), modify the lesson in these ways:

Alert #1: Ask for a volunteer to read the passage aloud.

Alert #2: Add this as a last debriefing question: *In what ways have you trusted Jesus and found him worthy of your trust? In what ways have you felt disappointed?*

CLOSING PRAYER

KNOW ME PRAYER

Time: about 10 minutes

Supplies: 1 penny or nickel for each child (to keep)

Give each child a penny or nickel. (If you're doing this activity in another country, adjust the activity to reflect a local coin.)

Say: **On the front of your coin you'll find a face. On the back of the coin is a building. And on the edge there's . . . well, nothing.**

We'll use our coins as prayer prompts to help us tell Jesus what's going on in our lives. I'll lead and then pause, giving you time to silently tell Jesus what you want him to know.

Yes, he already knows what's going on in our lives. But it's also true he wants a friendship with us—and friends tell each other what's happening!

First, please hold your coin so the face is up. Close your eyes and, for the next minute or two, tell Jesus about people in your life. Tell him about your friends (pause) **and about your family.** (pause) **Tell Jesus about people who aren't treating you well.** (pause)

Now turn your coin so the building is up. Tell Jesus what's happening in buildings in your life. Tell him about what's happening at the building where you go to school. (pause) **Tell Jesus about happenings in your home** (pause) **and at church.** (pause)

Now turn your coin so the edge is up. Tell Jesus what's keeping you on edge—worried—in your life. Maybe it's a test coming up or a friendship that's not happy. What is making you uncomfortable? (pause)

Close the prayer time by thanking Jesus for listening, for his friendship, and for being a good shepherd. Tell children to keep the coins as reminders to pray each time they see their coins during the coming week.

EXTRA-TIME ACTIVITY—OPTION 1

FAST FACTS

Time: about 10 minutes

Supplies: 1 sheet of paper and 1 pencil per child

Give each child a sheet of paper and a pencil. Ask children to write or draw their answers to the following questions—and not to show anyone their answers.

- ***What's your favorite pizza topping?***
- ***What's your favorite ice cream flavor?***
- ***What's your favorite sports team?***
- ***What's your favorite movie?***
- ***What's your favorite kind of dog?***
- ***Where were you born?***
- ***If you could paint your room any color, what would that color be?***

Collect and shuffle the papers. Then read several answers at a time from each paper. See how quickly kids can match up answers with names.

After playing, have kids circle up and discuss:

- ***How well do you think we know each other?***
- ***How well do you think Jesus knows us?***
- ***Is having Jesus know you a good thing or a bad thing? Why?***

EXTRA-TIME ACTIVITY—OPTION 2

WOLF ATTACK!

Time: about 5 minutes
Supplies: 1 sheet (or scrap) of paper per child

On each sheet of paper (except one) write the word *sheep*. On the last, write *wolf* (or draw sheep and a wolf, depending on the ages of kids). Fold the papers. Ask children to sit in a circle with a lot of space between them. Tell them these rules:

- **After I hand out the folded papers, wait to open them.**
- **When I give the signal, open your papers to see who you are. The "wolf" will try to touch as many "sheep" as possible in ten seconds. You sheep will scoot on your behinds to get away from the wolf.**

Hand out the papers at random and play several rounds. You'll play too! After playing, have children discuss:

- ***How would it feel to be a helpless sheep if a real wolf attacked?***
- ***What would a good shepherd do to help his sheep?***
- ***How does Jesus help you?***
- ***What makes it easy—or hard—to trust Jesus as your shepherd?***

EXTRA-TIME ACTIVITY—OPTION 3

INQUIRING MINDS WANT TO KNOW

Time: 5 minutes
Supplies: none

Gather kids in a circle. Ask: ***Imagine that you're all grown up and thinking back to this time. Who do you remember trusting? (like your grandma because she always told you the truth). What did you trust? (like the lock on the front door because it kept out bad guys). Was Jesus on your trust list? Why or why not?***

The Story of the Good Samaritan

The Point: We can help our neighbors.
Scripture Connect: Luke 10:30-37

Supplies for all Session 2 activities options: pencils, prepared poster, paper, safety scissors (several pairs), 1 marble per child, a few coins, 1 ball of yarn or string, the kids' socks and shoes, Bible, tape, 1 adhesive bandage per child, 1 sheet (or 2 for a larger group) of stiff paper or poster board (8½" x 11")

The Basics for Leaders

Jesus shared the story of the Good Samaritan as an answer to a question: "What should I do to inherit eternal life?" (Luke 10:25).

It's a straightforward question. So why didn't Jesus just answer it?

He did . . . but the man asking the question tried to wiggle out of doing what Jesus told him to do. The "loving God" part was fine—this man clearly cared about loving God. But the "taking care of neighbors" stuff? That was a problem.

The man wanted to know who Jesus considered as neighbors. And the answer clearly wasn't what the man wanted to hear: a neighbor is someone who needs your help.

It's still not a popular answer, but there it is. According to Jesus, your neighbor is anyone who needs you . . . and we can help our neighbors!

You'll help kids wrestle with that message today as you share this story—also known as a parable—of the Good Samaritan.

OPENING ACTIVITY—OPTION 1

HOWZITGOIN'

Time: about 5 minutes, depending on attendance
Supplies: pencils, prepared poster

Before kids arrive, draw a line on a poster. Place a 1 on the left end of the line, a 10 on the right, and a 5 in the middle. As kids arrive, ask them to pencil in their initials on the line.

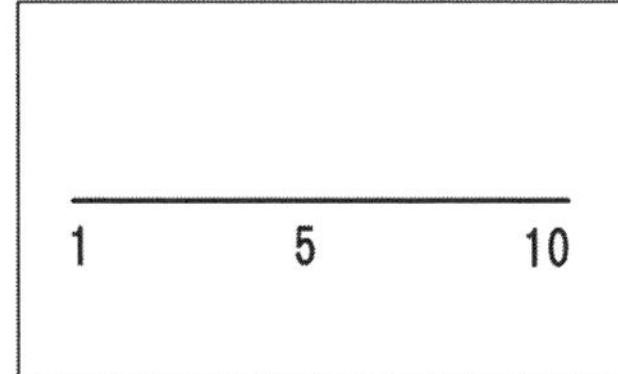

Say: **If this past week was so awful you wish you'd slept through it, place your initials by the 1. If it was a great week you wish you could repeat, put your initials by the 10. Place your initials anywhere on the line that shows how you feel about this past week—except exactly on the 5. That's because there's no such thing as a week that's exactly half good and half bad!**

After kids have signed in, give them 30 seconds each to explain why they placed their initials where they did. Be sure to include your own initials and explain your placement on the line. Kids will begin to express themselves more over time—and hearing their stories will help you adapt this lesson to make it relevant to your kids' lives.

OPENING ACTIVITY—OPTION 2

PAPER PEOPLE

Time: about 5 minutes, depending on attendance
Supplies: 1 sheet of paper and 1 pencil per child, safety scissors (several pairs)

Note: Since you will be using these paper dolls in the Cool Bible Story activity, be sure to have each child prepare one.

Ask children to cut out paper people that resemble the illustration. Encourage creativity—it's OK if the paper people don't all look the same.

Allow time for kids to trace and cut out their paper figures. If you have mostly younger kids, consider cutting out paper figures before this activity or trace the figures onto paper and let kids cut them out.

Say: **On your paper person, draw things that would make that person different from you. For example, it might be the person's skin color, shape of his or her eyes, hair style, or clothes. Or perhaps it's the person's age or attitude or even tattoos or gang signs. Draw anything that might cause you to think of the person as different from you.** (Make certain that kids draw on only one side of their paper figures.)

Allow time to finish drawing. Then ask children to introduce their paper people and explain what makes their people different or maybe even scary. If you've created a paper person (please do!), introduce yours as well.

Gather up the scissors, paper scraps, and the paper people. Set the paper people aside for the Cool Bible Story activity. Ask children to circle up and discuss:

- ***What are things that might make someone seem very different or even scary?***
- ***How often do you see someone like the person you drew?***
- ***That person you drew is your neighbor. True or false?***

Say: **When we think *neighbor* we think of people who live near us or are just like us. The people in Jesus' audience didn't like the Samaritans—who were different from them in many ways—and they didn't want to live with the Samaritans. But Jesus had a different meaning for the word *neighbor.* Let's explore a story Jesus told that had a very important meaning: our neighbor is anyone who needs us . . . and we can help our neighbors!**

Cool Story Game

Samaritan Sand Trap

Time: about 10 minutes

Supplies: pencils, 1 marble per child, a few coins, 1 ball of yarn or string, the kids' socks and shoes

Using yarn or string and the kids' shoes to create boundaries and socks as Samaritan Sand Traps, create a miniature golf course on the floor. Use shoes as additional golf course obstacles. For a "hole" use a coin. For best results create a course that takes a 90-degree turn about halfway through. Make one or more holes in your course, depending on materials, space, and time.

Explain the rules. Using a pencil as a golf club, each golfer will hit his or her marble in such a way that it stays on the course without crossing a boundary or touching a Samaritan Sand Trap. If either happens, the golfer will take a stroke and hit again from the spot where the marble went out of bounds.

Explain the goal. Complete the course without going off the path . . . or touching a Samaritan! The course is considered completed when each golfer's marble has touched the coin and been removed from the course.

Play several rounds, moving around the socks, if desired. When you're finished, gather the marbles and pencils and have kids put their socks and shoes back on.

Say: **In our game we didn't want to be near the Samaritans . . . and we didn't help each other. In the story Jesus told, some of the people didn't like each other and some didn't help others. Let's see how many other ways our game was like Jesus' story!**

Cool BIBLE STORY

PAPER PUPPETS

Time: about 15 minutes

Supplies: Bible, tape, paper people from Opening Activity—Option 2

Gather children in a circle. Place in the center of the circle the paper people you made earlier. Ask each child to reclaim his or her paper person. Hold the tape beside you.

Say: **Jesus told a story about someone whom Jewish people usually hated: a Samaritan man. To Jewish people, Samaritans were different and maybe even a bit scary. The side of your paper person that has a drawing on it will be the Samaritan man.** Ask children to turn their paper people over and look at the blank sides.

Say: **Your blank paper person is the other person in this story: a Jewish man walking on a road, out in the country. Our story begins with the Jewish man, so look at the blank side of your paper person. As I read the story Jesus told, please act out the story using your paper people. I'll make some suggestions, but you can add your own actions too.**

Read aloud Luke 10:30-37. Suggestions for actions are indicated below.

- verse 30: Crumple the paper figures. Add several small tears and then toss the paper people out of reach, back into the center of the circle.
- verse 31: Turn your heads to the left to avoid seeing the paper people.
- verse 32: Turn your heads to the right to avoid seeing the paper people.
- verse 33. Retrieve the paper people and smooth them out; hold them so the Samaritan side is facing up.
- verse 34: Use tape to repair any tears.
- verse 35: Ask kids to pretend to empty their pockets and give a couple of coins to you.

After the story, applaud your actors. Then ask kids to sit and discuss:

- ***Tell about a time you helped someone. What did you do to help?***
- ***Why are we sometimes slow to help others?***
- ***What can we learn from Jesus' story about the Samaritan?***

Say: **There are so many people we can help, including our family members, friends, neighbors, and even others at church. If someone needs help and we're there, that person is our neighbor—and we can help him or her!**

CLOSING PRAYER

NEIGHBORLY PRAYER

Time: about 10 minutes

Supplies: 1 adhesive bandage per child

Give each child an adhesive bandage. Say: **Bandages remind us of healing and helping, don't they? In our Bible story, we learned how a man helped his hurt neighbor. You can hold your bandage as we pray and ask God to help us think of people we can help too.**

Ask children to close their eyes. Pray: **Dear God, thank you for helping us just as the Good Samaritan helped the wounded man on the road. You've treated us with kindness when we didn't deserve it. You've helped us by sending Jesus to forgive our sins. You've given us hope when we feel sad or alone. In every way, you have loved and helped us.**

There are people who can use our help too. Pray for one person you know at school or at home who is hurting or sad. Maybe you know the person's name. Maybe you just kind of know the person. Who needs you to be a Good Samaritan? Pause for children to silently pray.

Now ask God how you could be of help. Maybe it's just a smile. Maybe it's talking with the person. Maybe it's helping the person make new friends. Ask God what you can do to be a Good Samaritan. (pause)

Now silently open your eyes and open your bandage. Without talking, place your bandage on the back of your hand to remember the person you thought of. If any children need help with opening the bandages, silently provide it.

Close the prayer time by thanking God for bringing to mind people who need your help, just as you've needed God's help. Finish by discussing the following questions:

- ***Who came to mind as you prayed?***
- ***What might you do to be a Good Samaritan to that person?***
- ***What might happen if you're helpful? if you aren't?***
- ***What could make it hard to help that person?***

√ Say: **It was hard for the Samaritan who helped the wounded man too. What if the Samaritan had been blamed for the crime? What would the other Samaritans think of him helping out a Jew? And what if the cost of the wounded man's care was really high?**

√ **None of that mattered. What mattered was that being a neighbor means caring for those who need help—no matter who they are.**

EXTRA-TIME ACTIVITY—OPTION 1

DISAPPEARING NEIGHBORS

Time: about 10 minutes

Supplies: 1 sheet (or 2 for a larger group) of stiff paper or poster board (8½" x 11")

Prepare a small poster by placing an *N* on the left and an *S* on the right of the paper. If you have just a few children, one poster will be enough. Four or more kids? Make two, and you'll keep anyone from waiting too long for a turn during the activity.

Have children do this:

1. **Hold the poster a foot from your nose with the *S* to the right.**
2. **Cover your right eye and look at the *S* with your left eye.**
3. **Move the poster slowly away, straight ahead, staying focused on the *S*.**

At some point the *N* will disappear from view! Be sure each child has a turn making the *N* disappear.

When everyone has had a turn, say: **Think of the letter *S* as standing for *self*—meaning ourselves. You can think of the *N* as your *neighbor*.** Ask:

- ***What happens to the* N *when we focus on the* S*? In other words, what happens to our neighbors when we focus only on ourselves?***
- ***Do you think it's wise to never focus on our neighbors, but only on ourselves? Explain.***

Say: **Here's the truth: When we focus only on ourselves, sooner or later**

our neighbors disappear—they stop mattering. We quit seeing them.

Jesus' story about the Good Samaritan is a reminder that when our neighbors need us, we've got to be there, ready to help. We can show them the same love Jesus shows us!

EXTRA-TIME ACTIVITY—OPTION 2

POSTSCRIPT

Time: about 5 minutes
Supplies: none

Help kids form pairs. Ask the person in each pair who's wearing the most black and blue (the color of bruises!) to be the Wounded Man. The other person in each pair will be the Good Samaritan.

Say: **Wounded Man, let's say you're at the inn and you're all healed up. The Samaritan who helped you has come to see you. What will you say to him? Tell him now.** After kids have turns telling what they would say, ask:

- ***Saying "thank you" is fine—but what else would you say to someone who helped you so much?***
- ***In what ways has Jesus helped you?***
- ***What would you say to Jesus for helping you?***

EXTRA-TIME ACTIVITY—OPTION 3

INQUIRING MINDS WANT TO KNOW

Time: 5 minutes
Supplies: none

Gather kids in a circle. Ask: ***Does Jesus really expect us to help everyone who needs help? How can we do that much?***

SESSION 3

The Story of the Vineyard

The Point: Life's not fair—but God is always loving.
Scripture Connect: Matthew 20:1-15

Supplies for all Session 3 activities options: pencils, prepared poster, paper, masking tape, Bible, 1 small sack or basket, treats or favors (1 per child), 1 cup or basket, 10 coins per child (you'll get them back!)

The Basics for Leaders

Jesus spent a lot of time explaining a very basic truth to his audiences. The kingdom of God isn't just about rules or about behavior or about justice. It's also about grace.

Jesus told this story to help his audience grab hold of a basic truth: God is generous, and his gifts of salvation and eternal life are available to anyone who believes in him and trusts him—whether that belief comes at the beginning of a long life or just moments before someone dies.

Something about that arrangement doesn't seem fair to us. We want a bonus for spending a lifetime serving God. And in believing this, we miss the same three points that the people who heard Jesus' story (or parable) missed:

1. God gives us a wonderful gift, just as he promised.
2. It's up to God if he decides to be generous with others.
3. Having a lifetime serving God is a bonus!

You'll help your kids discover these truths today as you share the story of the workers in the vineyard.

OPENING ACTIVITY—OPTION 1

HOWZITGOIN'

Time: about 5 minutes, depending on attendance
Supplies: pencils, prepared poster

Before kids arrive, draw a line on a poster. Place a 1 on the left end of the line, a 10 on the right, and a 5 in the middle. As kids arrive, ask them to pencil in their initials on the line.

1 5 10

Say: **If this past week was so awful you wish you'd slept through it, place your initials by the 1. If it was a great week you wish you could repeat, put your initials by the 10. Place your initials anywhere on the line that shows how you feel about this past week—except exactly on the 5. That's because there's no such thing as a week that's exactly half good and half bad!**

After kids have signed in, give them 30 seconds each to explain why they placed their initials where they did. Be sure to include your own initials and explain your placement on the line. Kids will begin to express themselves more over time—and hearing their stories will help you adapt this lesson to make it relevant to your kids' lives.

OPENING ACTIVITY—OPTION 2

PUPPY-SITTING FLUFFY

Time: about 10 minutes
Supplies: 1 sheet of paper and 1 pencil per child

Form children into pairs and hand each child a sheet of paper and a pencil. Ask children to decide who in each pair will be the Day Person and who will be the Night Person.

Say: **Let's say I'll be out of town and need someone to care for my puppy. I'll be gone 24 hours, and I'll pay someone to care for little Fluffy.**

Before you decide if you want the job, let's list all of the things you need to do to care for a puppy during the day and night. The Day Person in each pair will list what it takes to care for Fluffy during the day, and the Night Person will list what it takes to care for Fluffy during the night.

As kids make suggestions, have them write the tasks on their papers. Be specific, making sure all tasks happen during the day. Explain that Fluffy sleeps from 8:00 PM to 8:00 AM and doesn't have "accidents," so there's really nothing to do at night.

AGE-ALERT TIPS

If you have mostly **younger children** who may not be able to list items, encourage them to act out their jobs. If a child is the Day Person, he or she might act out feeding and giving water to the puppy as well as taking the puppy for walks. The child playing the Night Person will simply act out sleeping. This will help younger kids see how unfair the payments are for puppy-sitting!

When the lists are complete, have kids read them aloud. Then say: **I'll pay $100 for Fluffy's care, but I want to hire a team of two people—one to handle the day and the other to handle the night. I'll pay your team $100. What's a fair way for you to split the money? Splitting the money right down the middle, with $50 each, isn't fair because the Day Person is doing all the work. How would you split it?** Give pairs time to talk, and then ask them to share with the larger group their split solutions. Ask:

- ***How did you decide what was fair?***
- ***How would each Day Person feel if the Night Person got paid the same amount?***

Say: **Today we're diving into a story Jesus told that's much like what we just did. People were hired to work, but not all of them were happy with how they were paid.**

The people listening to Jesus' story discovered what we'll discover: life's not fair, but God is always loving!

Cool Story Game

Fair Teams

Time: about 10 minutes

Supplies: masking tape

Place a masking tape line on the floor to separate the playing area into two sections. Tell kids to form two teams for Piggyback Races. Have each team stand on one side of the line.

When kids are in place, say: **We're not really going to have Piggyback Races, but I'm curious. How did you choose your teams? Was it because of size, height, weight, or age? Did this make fair teams? Why or why not?**

Encourage kids to tell how they chose up their teams, and if this made them fair. Then say: **People say life should be fair. Let's see how well that works. We'll form teams for a few pretend games and see if we can make the teams exactly, absolutely, completely fair.**

When I call out a type of game, you'll have 60 seconds to choose teams, one team on each side of the line. Make the teams fair and be able to explain why after each round. Ready?

Pick fair teams for a . . .

- Kitty-petting contest
- Dance contest
- Juggling contest
- Handwriting contest
- Relay race
- Spelling bee
- Staring contest
- Skipping contest

After each round, ask how kids decided what would make teams fair. Is it age? numbers? experience? strength? Push for specifics.

Say: **Hard to make teams fair, huh? We're all different and all good at different things. But God knows us all, and knows what we need. And though life isn't always fair, God loves us all! Jesus told a parable (or story) about a vineyard where grapes are grown, and about a boss who seemed unfair to his workers. Let's explore that story now!**

Cool BIBLE STORY

FAIR OR NOT?

Time: about 15 minutes

Supplies: Bible, 1 small sack or basket, treats or favors (1 per child)

Before children arrive, place small treats or favors in a sack or basket. Consider using small erasers, new pencils, or individually wrapped candies.

Invite children to form three groups. Remember, one child can be a group if necessary. Have groups sit on the floor. Hold the treat sack or basket. Explain that you have treats to share. But to receive them, groups need to do some work. Ask the first group to stand up and sit down 15 times—quickly—to get their treats. Have everyone count along out loud.

When the first group has completed the task, announce that the second group has to do the same thing—6 times—to earn a prize. Have everyone count aloud. Say: **We have one last group. How many stand-up-sit-downs should they do? 35? 47? How about . . . 1?**

When the last group has accomplished its task, give everyone one treat from the sack. Then have kids sit in place and discuss:

- ***Was it fair that some of you worked harder and still got the same reward? Explain.***
- ***Are rewards always fair? Why or why not?***

Say: **Jesus told a story about a vineyard where grapes are grown, and about a boss and his workers. Let's read the story aloud. As you listen, see whether you think the boss's payment to the workers was fair or unfair, loving or unkind.**

Read aloud Matthew 20:1-12. Invite older kids to take turns reading aloud if they'd like. When you finish reading the passage, ask:

- ***Do you think the boss was fair or unfair? Explain.***
- ***In what ways can something or someone seem unfair, but still be kind and loving?***

Read aloud Matthew 20:13-15. Then ask:

- ***Would you rather someone in charge be fair or loving? Explain.***
- ***Would you rather God be absolutely fair or loving? Explain.***

Say: **God is fair . . . *and* loving. And it's a good thing for us that he's loving, because if he gave us what we deserve, we'd all be in trouble. Romans 3:23 says that we've all sinned and disappointed God.** If you have older kids, read aloud Romans 6:23 to remind them of God's loving grace through Jesus.

Say: **Good news, though: God sent Jesus to save us!** Read aloud Romans 5:8. Then say: **Life isn't always fair, but God is always loving. And for that we can be deeply thankful!**

CLOSING PRAYER

THUMBNAIL PRAYER

Time: about 5 minutes
Supplies: 1 cup or basket, 10 coins per child (you'll get them back)

Raid your piggy bank. You'll give each child at least ten coins. Be clear you'd like the coins back.

Explain to children that in a few moments they'll stack coins on their thumbs. Say: **Hold your hand in a fist like this** (demonstrate) **with your thumbnail up. Stack as many coins on your thumbs as you can. How many you can stack depends on how flat your thumbnail is, how steady your hand is, and how big your thumb is. You may be a one-coin stacker or a ten-coin stacker. It all depends. Let's give it a try.**

Once children have finished stacking coins, say: **Hey—it's not fair if someone has a flatter thumb than you—or a bigger thumb! Life's not fair!**

Ask children to very slowly open their hands while keeping their coin stacks standing on their thumbs. It's hard—some stacks will tumble!

Say: **It's not fair that some of us have steadier hands than others. Life's not fair!** Collect all but one coin from each child. Say: **Life's not fair, but no matter how God made your thumb, he loves you. He loves us all—whether we're one-coin or ten-coin stackers!** Ask children to each hold their coins in their palms with palms up and open.

Pray and thank God for loving us no matter what. Thank him that he hasn't made us all the same. Thank God that he treats us with love and grace, not just punishing us for doing what he says is wrong. Invite kids to take turns thanking God for his love.

When children have finished praying, ask them to drop their coins in the cup or basket as a sign of thanking God for his love.

EXTRA-TIME ACTIVITY—OPTION 1

STAND UP. SIT DOWN

Time: about 5 minutes
Supplies: none

If time

Seat kids on the floor. Say: **Life's not fair. Some of us are good at one thing and not another. But we're all good at something—God has given us each at least one talent or gift we can use to help others and to praise God.**

I'll call out a list of things we may be good at, or enjoy doing even if we're not yet all-stars. If something I mention describes you, jump up—then quickly sit down.

Read this list and add items you know will touch on what your kids enjoy doing. Read quickly with just a brief pause between items: reader, writer, runner, singer, actor, dancer, scientist, mountain climber, room cleaner, math whiz, hiker, biker, kite flyer, painter, ice-cream eater, and—ta-dah!—list reader.

Say: **Good job! What's something else you enjoy doing?** After kids make suggestions, say: **Life's not fair. We aren't all good at the same things. But isn't it great that God made us all different? And that he loves us?**

EXTRA-TIME ACTIVITY—OPTION 2

RULES. RULES. RULES

Time: about 10 minutes
Supplies: 1 sheet of paper and 1 pencil per child

Ask children to write or draw (or simply discuss) what they feel is the right punishment for each of the broken house rules listed below. Then have kids share their answers.

- Trashing the house and refusing to clean up
- Saying, "Yuk! I won't eat this slop!" when dinner is served
- Blaming someone else for something you did
- Not doing schoolwork and lying about it later

Say: **Wow—sounds like punishments are different in different homes. Is that fair?**

Parents don't always respond the same way to situations. But something they pretty much have in common is that they love us enough to discipline us and help us behave properly. They may not always be fair, but they always love us!

(Note: Be on the lookout if a child describes an over-the-top punishment, perhaps even abuse. If that's the case, tell someone in authority, such as your pastor or children's pastor. Don't use this as an excuse for gossip, but do let someone appropriate know your concerns.)

AGE-ALERT TIPS

If you have **younger children**, explain what the word *punishment* means. Remind them that even though we sometimes make wrong choices and receive punishments, God still loves us—and loves it when we tell him we're sorry!

EXTRA-TIME ACTIVITY—OPTION 3

INQUIRING MINDS WANT TO KNOW

Time: 5 minutes
Supplies: none

Gather kids in a circle. Ask: ***Describe a time at school that something didn't seem fair. How did you feel? Describe a time something wasn't fair—but you came out ahead. How did you feel then?***

SESSION 4

The Story of the Lost Coin

The Point: God wants you—a lot!
Scripture Connect: Luke 15:8-10

Supplies for all Session 4 activities options: pencils, prepared poster, 1 quarter, electrical or duct tape, 1 bucket, several trays of ice cubes, newspapers, paper towels, Bibles, paper, 10 pennies (kids will keep these)

The Basics for Leaders

Religious leaders in Jesus' day were upset to see Jesus hanging around with people who had bad reputations—including tax collectors.

Tax collectors at that time deserved their bad reputations. They worked for the Romans, the army that had conquered their country. Tax collectors made money by taking more money from citizens than Rome required.

The result: tax collectors got rich—by stealing.

Jesus told this story about a lost coin to make a point: that he came to seek and save lost people—even terrible sinners like tax collectors. And when a sinner came to God, there was a celebration just like when the woman found her lost coin.

That's how much your kids are worth. That's what you're worth. Help each of your children hear this message loud and clear: God wants us—a lot!

OPENING ACTIVITY—OPTION 1

HOWZITGOIN'

Time: about 5 minutes, depending on attendance
Supplies: pencils, prepared poster

Before kids arrive, draw a line on a poster. Place a 1 on the left end of the line, a 10 on the right, and a 5 in the middle. As kids arrive, ask them to pencil in their initials on the line.

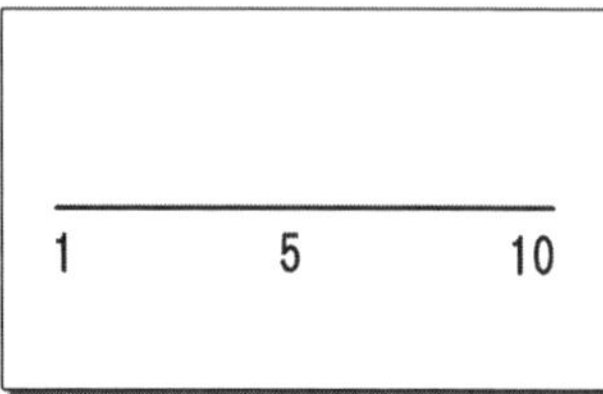

Say: **If this past week was so awful you wish you'd slept through it, place your initials by the 1. If it was a great week you wish you could repeat, put your initials by the 10. Place your initials anywhere on the line that shows how you feel about this past week—except exactly on the 5. That's because there's no such thing as a week that's exactly half good and half bad!**

After kids have signed in, give them 30 seconds each to explain why they placed their initials where they did. Be sure to include your own initials and explain your placement on the line. Kids will begin to express themselves more over time—and hearing their stories will help you adapt this lesson to make it relevant to your kids' lives.

OPENING ACTIVITY—OPTION 2

HOTTER-COLDER RESCUE MISSION

Time: about 5 minutes, depending on attendance
Supplies: 1 quarter, electrical or duct tape

Before children arrive, tape a quarter to the bottom of your shoe using electrical or duct tape. Be careful not to let children see the sole of your shoe or discover that you've taped something there.

Ask kids to stand in a circle facing outward. Then ask them to link elbows so that every child has both elbows linked.

Say: **In a few moments you'll move around, but you'll do so as a single unit—as one group. I've hidden a coin in this room and as you move together, I'll tell you if you're getting hotter or colder in finding the coin. Your job is to rescue the coin. There are three rules:**

1. You can't unlink elbows.

2. I'll only say *hotter* or *colder* once every 15 seconds.

3. It's not enough to guess where the coin is. You have to actually pick it up to rescue it and set it free—without unlinking elbows.

As children move around the room in response to your prompts of hotter/colder, feel free to move too. Be helpful by joining the children as they search in a closet or check under a rug.

Once kids have caught on and cornered you so you can lift a foot to have them remove the tape, ask them to sit in a circle on the floor—facing inward. Ask children to discuss:

- ***What kept you looking for the coin so you could rescue it?***
- ***Why do you think Jesus keeps looking for people to rescue them?***
- ***In what ways has Jesus looked for you?***

Say: **Today we'll dive into a story Jesus told about a lost coin. There's a message in this story for us. Let's see if we can find it!**

Cool Story Game

Done Lost It!

Time: 10 minutes or more, as desired

Supplies: 1 bucket, several trays of ice cubes, 1 quarter, newspapers, paper towels

Place several trays of ice in a bucket and set the bucket on newspapers in the playing area. In this game, you'll hide the quarter in the bucket each round, so plan on some frosty fingers.

Form children into pairs. Tell kids the goal of the game is for them to each scrounge around in the bucket to retrieve a shiny quarter. The challenge: they have to find the quarter in the midst of a bunch of ice cubes while someone else is trying to find it too—and all without looking!

As the ice melts, you may wish to add more to the bucket. The more ice you add, the harder it is to find the quarter.

Give each pair up to 60 seconds to find the coin before moving to the next pair. Give every pair a few paper towels to dry their icy fingers!

After each pair has taken a turn (or more than one—it's up to you), have children sit in a circle and discuss:

- ***What made finding the quarter difficult or easy?***
- ***What do you think makes it difficult for Jesus to reach others? easy to reach them?***

Say: **We'll explore a story today about a woman who didn't give up when she was searching for a lost coin. She looked everywhere in her home until at last she found it. There's a message in this story for us to discover too! Let's take a look!**

Cool BIBLE STORY

MONEY MUSIC

Time: about 20 minutes

Supplies: Bible, 1 sheet of paper and 1 pencil per child

Even if you're not a musician, you can sing the ever-popular ditty "My Bonnie." Admit it: you know the tune and, more importantly, so do your kids.

Today you'll please the more musical among your kids as they pair up to write a new verse called "My Money."

Ask children to form pairs. Give each child a sheet of paper and pencil.

Say: **Jesus told a story about a woman who lost a coin—a silver coin—one of only ten she had. The value of the coin, which was a *drachma*, was high: about a full day's pay for a worker. Let's see how she reacted to her loss.**

Ask a capable reader among your children to read aloud Luke 15:8.

Say: **There are two clues that this woman was poor. First, she had just ten coins. Second, she had to light a lamp to find her coin. That meant her house had no windows or natural light, which a more expensive house would have had.**

So what did she do? She looked for the coin! Let's write some coin-hunting music for her.

Ask children to sing with you the first verse and chorus of "My Bonnie." Then sing the following sample verse and chorus of "My Money" (or if you simply can't bring yourself to sing the words, just say them).

My money lies under the sofa,
My money went straight down the sink.
My money is missing, so tell me,
Where is my money, you think?
Bring back, bring back,
Bring back my money to me, to me!
Bring back, bring back,
Bring back my money to me!

AGE-ALERT TIPS

Let **younger kids** draw simple pictures of where they would look for the lost coin.

After singing, give pairs several minutes to work together writing their own verses and indicating where they'd look for a coin in their houses. Then ask children to share their verses. No verses written? Ask children to just tell where they'd look.

Continue by reading aloud Luke 15:9, 10. Ask writing partners to discuss:

- ***Why did Jesus tell this story?***
- ***Why do you suppose angels are happy when people come to God?***
- ***Why do you think God wants a friendship with us?***

Say: **God gave us his laws. He sent prophets to tell us what he wanted. He sent his Son to save us. He left his Holy Spirit to help us. God wants us—*a lot*! The question is: do we want him too? Of course we do!**

CLOSING PRAYER

HIDE-AND-SEEK PRAYER

Time: about 5 minutes
Supplies: none

Ask each child to hide someplace in the immediate area. As you call each child's name, ask that child to join you in the middle of the room. Thank God for choosing to find and love him or her. Then offer each child a chance to add their own thank-you prayers to God, if desired.

If you're in a room where there's no place to hide, do this: Stand in the center of the room and close your eyes. Invite children to each take a spot in the room and then, as you sweep the room pointing, offer a series of short prayers. The child nearest to where you're pointing each time can consider himself the one being prayed for.

Close by thanking God for seeking and finding you too.

AGE-ALERT TIPS

Both **younger** *and* **older kids** are often too shy to pray aloud for a group. If your kids are too shy to pray aloud, ask them to join you in the center of the room as you call their names. Then finish by having everyone hold hands as you offer a prayer.

EXTRA-TIME ACTIVITY—OPTION 1

42-SECOND TREASURE HUNT

Time: about 10 minutes
Supplies: 10 pennies (kids will keep these)

Before kids arrive, hide ten pennies in the room where you'll be meeting. Tell your children about the ten pennies. Explain that they'll have exactly 42 seconds to find the coins. What they find, they can keep. Tell kids that if they move something to look beneath or behind it, they must return that item to the original position.

After the treasure hunt, say: **You worked hard looking for just one penny. The woman who lost her coin in our Bible story had a coin worth far more—about a day's pay—so imagine how hard she looked!**

Here's good news: you're more precious to God than that coin was to the woman in our story. God wants a friendship with you so much that he sent Jesus to help bring you close to him. God wants you—a lot!

EXTRA-TIME ACTIVITY—OPTION 2

SEARCH AND RESCUE

Time: about 10 minutes
Supplies: 1 Bible for every 2 children

This activity works best with older elementary children who find it easy to read—but if you use a kid-friendly version, these passages are also appropriate for younger children. With younger children, plan to read the passages aloud and discuss the meaning as a group.

Form children into pairs and give each a Bible. (Just a few children? No problem—each child can look up a passage.) Have pairs find and read these passages: Luke 19:10; John 3:16, 17; 2 Peter 3:8-10; Romans 8:38, 39. Help children use the table of contents in their Bibles to find the passages.

After children read, have them summarize what they read in their own words for the larger group. Then discuss:

- ***What does this passage tell us about Jesus wanting us—a lot?***
- ***What does Jesus want to do with us? How do we feel about that?***
- ***What happens if we work together with Jesus?***

EXTRA-TIME ACTIVITY—OPTION 3

INQUIRING MINDS WANT TO KNOW

Time: 5 minutes
Supplies: none

Gather kids in a circle. Ask: ***What possession, if you lost it, would you turn your house upside down to search for? Why is the item worth so much to you? Why do you think we are so precious to God?***

SESSION **5**

The Story of the Found Son

The Point: God is forgiving.
Scripture Connect: Luke 15:11-32

Supplies for all Session 5 activities options: pencils, prepared poster, paper, tape, safety scissors (several pairs), 5 coins per child (you'll get them back), 1 wastebasket, 1 towel, Bible, 1 oven mitt, 1 newspaper page per child

The Basics for Leaders

This story is one of a series Jesus told to help people know God and to help them realize how eager God is to welcome them into the kingdom.

How eager is that? Well, it's eager enough to forgive people who speak poorly of God and take advantage of his kindness. If they repent and if they turn away from the bad things they've done and ask for forgiveness, then he's willing to forgive them. That's the meaning of this well-known story. God is forgiving—and it's the truth you'll help your children discover!

OPENING ACTIVITY—OPTION 1

HOWZITGOIN'

Time: about 5 minutes, depending on attendance
Supplies: pencils, prepared poster

Before kids arrive, draw a line on a poster. Place a 1 on the left end of the line, a 10 on the right, and a 5 in the middle. As kids arrive, ask them to pencil in their initials on the line.

Say: **If this past week was so awful you wish you'd slept through it, place your initials by the 1. If it was a great week you wish you could repeat, put your initials by the 10. Place your initials anywhere on the line that shows how you feel about this past week—except exactly on the 5. That's because there's no such thing as a week that's exactly half good and half bad!**

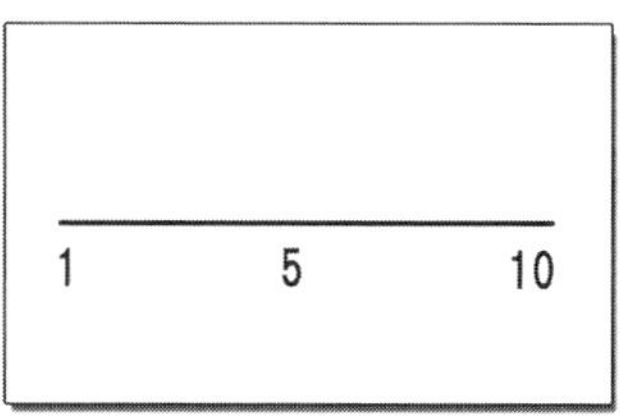

After kids have signed in, give them 30 seconds each to explain why they placed their initials where they did. Be sure to include your own initials and explain your placement on the line. Kids will begin to express themselves more over time—and hearing their stories will help you adapt this lesson to make it relevant to your kids' lives.

OPENING ACTIVITY—OPTION 2

GOD'S FORGIVENESS STRIP

Time: about 10 minutes

Supplies: paper, 1 pencil per child, tape, safety scissors (several pairs)

Note: You'll use these strips for the Closing Prayer activity, so be sure each child makes one. Before children arrive, cut 2" x 11" strips of paper. Cut one or two strips per child. Practice the steps outlined below so you're able to give kids clear directions in completing the project. (Technically, this is called a Mobius strip, but we're going to call it God's Forgiveness Strip.)

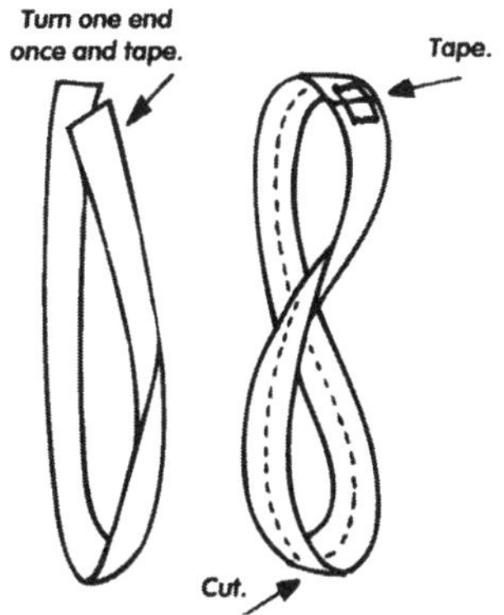

Give each child a strip of paper and a pencil. (Younger children will need extra help with this activity. Consider pairing them with older kids.) Use pencils to write "God's Forgiveness Strip" on the strips of paper. Bring the ends of each strip together as if creating a paper circle, but give one end a half twist. Tape the ends of the circle. Use tape on both sides where the paper ends join.

Show children how to poke their scissors carefully through the centers of the strips and cut down the centers, continuing all the way around the circles. As you help the children, ask them what they think will happen as they complete the cut.

Surprise! Kids won't have two circles. Instead, they'll have a longer loop.

Collect the strips and set them aside as you have children sit in a circle on the floor. Discuss:

- ***How do you know God forgives you?***
- ***If you walked away from God, would he welcome you back? Why?***

Say: **The loop you made is like God's forgiveness—it never ends. In a story Jesus told, a young man learned that his father's love didn't end either, even though he walked away from his father. Let's see what happened when the young man turned around and went home again.**

Cool Story Game

Wasting Money

Time: 10 minutes or more, as desired

Supplies: 5 coins per child (you'll get them back), 1 wastebasket, 1 towel

Say: **In our story today we'll learn how a young man wasted a lot of money in what the Bible calls "wild living." What might a person do today that we would call wild living?** Suggestions might include spending money on foolish things, driving too fast, drinking too much, buying and using drugs, and getting arrested.

Say: **We don't know exactly what he did with his father's money, but he managed to lose it all. Not that I want you to get good at doing the same thing, but let's practice throwing away a bit of money now.**

Place a wastebasket 10 feet from the children. Place a towel inside the basket to dull the sound of coins landing. Toss coins, one at a time, toward the basket. Older children can flip their coins—it adds even more challenge.

As they toss the coins, tell them to call out what they'd buy with each coin if it was worth $100. Because children don't know what most things cost, be prepared for interesting answers!

When children have finished, have them help you collect stray coins and drop them in the wastebasket. Then ask children to stand in a circle around the basket. Say: **Suppose this wasn't your money to waste but belonged to your parents. How happy do you think they'd be to see you when you came home and announced you'd thrown away $500?**

Allow children to respond. Then say: **That's what happened to a young man in a story Jesus told. He took his father's money and threw it away by making really bad choices. Then he wanted to come home again. Let's find out what happened to him!**

AGE-ALERT TIPS

Alert #1: If you have lots of **younger kids**, simply place the wastebasket closer.

Alert #2: Invite **older children** to toss their coins from a greater distance.

Cool BIBLE STORY

MOVE THE MITT!

Time: about 20 minutes
Supplies: Bible, 1 oven mitt

Gather children in a circle and place the oven mitt in the middle of the circle. Explain that oven mitts are used to handle very hot things—and today that hot thing is anger.

Say: **As we read a story that Jesus told, we'll decide as a group who has the right to be angry. That person will wear this oven mitt.**

Assign three roles: father, younger son, and older son. Everyone else will play the part of the pigs. Very few children? No problem! Take on the role of older son yourself and assign just the father and younger son roles.

Invite the kids playing the role of the pigs to practice their sound effects a few times. Then ask for silence and begin reading. Read aloud Luke 15: 11, 12. Say: **Money wasn't handed out to sons until fathers died. The younger son is saying, "I wish you were dead so I could get my money." Who has a right to be angry here?** (Father—let the father put on the mitt.)

Read verses 13-15. Ask:

- ***Does the younger son have a right to be angry about running out of money?*** (No—so keep the mitt on the father.)

Read verse 16 aloud. Ask:

- ***Do the pigs have the right to be angry about having only crummy food to eat?*** (No—but don't put it to a vote!)

Read verses 17-24 aloud. Ask:

- ***What did the father do with his right to be angry?*** (He gave it up—so have the father take off the mitt and place it on the floor.)

Read verses 25-32 aloud. Ask:

- ***Does the older son have the right to be angry?*** (No. He'll receive what's due him, as promised. He doesn't get to wear the mitt!)

Say: **In this story there were plenty of mistakes made. And yet the only one who had a right to be angry was the father—and he chose to forgive his younger son.** As a large group discuss:

- ***In what ways are we like the younger son?***
- ***In what ways are we like the older son?***
- ***In what ways, if any, are we like the father?***

Say: **When we forgive we give up the right to be angry. We choose to be happy even when life isn't fair. We let go of our hurt feelings. It's easier when people like the younger son ask for forgiveness, but it's our choice. We can forgive others even when they don't deserve it. That's what God has done with us. We don't deserve it, but God is forgiving!**

CLOSING PRAYER

GOD-IS-FORGIVING PRAYER

Time: about 5 minutes

Supplies: God's Forgiveness Strips from Opening Activity—Option 2

Hand each child the God's Forgiveness Strip that he or she made earlier. Ask children to place both hands through their strips and clasp their hands together.

Say: **When the father in Jesus' story had the chance to have his son come back—even after the son had done things that the older son thought were unforgivable—the father jumped at the chance. His son was more important than the lost money, his pride, or others' anger at him for being so forgiving. The father just wanted his son back. That's what mattered.**

God's forgiveness is like that. It surrounds us. Like the paper circle, it's eternal—it goes and goes without any end. Let's thank God for his forgiveness and love.

Ask children to offer out-loud prayers, thanking God for his love and forgiveness. After letting kids pray silently, close the prayer for your group. Collect the God's Forgiveness Strips to hand out when kids leave.

EXTRA-TIME ACTIVITY—OPTION 1

NEWSPAPER PAINS

Time: about 10 minutes

Supplies: 1 newspaper page per child

Have children fold their newspaper pages in half. Ask them to hold the papers at arm's length, using both hands and keeping the papers straight in front of them.

Say: **How heavy or light would you say your newspaper page is? Pretty light, right? It's not hard at all to hold it out in front of you . . . elbows locked . . . straight ahead. But keep holding it.**

Ask children to keep the papers in the same position for 90 seconds without talking. It will seem like an eternity to them.

After 90 seconds, say: **How heavy does the paper feel now? Heavier, huh?** Ask children to drop their arms and shake out the cramps. Collect the newspaper pages. Then say: **When we've done something wrong, it's like** carrying a weight. Even a little weight gets heavy if we hold it a long time. But when we ask God for forgiveness, he takes the weight from us. We don't have to carry it anymore! That's not just good news . . . it's great news. God is forgiving!**

EXTRA-TIME ACTIVITY—OPTION 2

FEAST!

Time: about 5 minutes
Supplies: 1 sheet of paper and 1 pencil per child

Give each child one sheet of paper and a pencil. Ask children to draw a dinner plate on their papers and then, on the plate, the food they'd most want to see at a feast in their honor. After children explain what they have on their plates, discuss:

- ***Why do you think the father in Jesus' story served such expensive food?***
- ***Who was happy when you decided to be in a friendship with God? Or haven't you made that decision yet?***

Say: **All of us come to God in the same way: by feeling his love and asking for his forgiveness. And God's answer is always the same: to forgive us**!

EXTRA-TIME ACTIVITY—OPTION 3

INQUIRING MINDS WANT TO KNOW

Time: 5 minutes
Supplies: none

Gather kids in a circle. Ask: ***Who have you forgiven? How did it feel to forgive someone else? How does it feel to know you've been forgiven by God?***

SESSION **6**

The Story of the Ten Talents

The Point: Use your talents to serve God.
Scripture Connect: Matthew 25:14-29

Supplies for all Session 6 activities options: pencils, prepared poster, 1 apple per child (and a few extras), paper towels, 1 bowl of water, 2 or 3 rubber bands per child, newspapers, Bible, paper, 1 bowl

The Basics for Leaders

When Jesus first told his stories, or parables, his audience understood the words he used. Over time, some of those words have been used differently. This is one of those times.

The word *talent* in Jesus' day referred to money, not abilities. The amount a talent was worth varied throughout the years and from location to location, but it's possible that at this time a talent was worth about 6,000 days' wages—at least 15 years' salary for an average worker. That's a lot of money, so even the servant in this story who got just one talent was given a great deal of responsibility.

Also in Jesus' time, a slave might be a well-educated person who had fallen on hard times and had to sell himself or herself. A rich Roman in the first century might own a teacher or a doctor as a slave. Trusting slaves with money wasn't uncommon.

How we use the abilities God has given us isn't the original point of this story, but it is one way to apply it. And that's what you'll help your kids understand today: that no matter what God has given them, including money, they should use their talents for God.

OPENING ACTIVITY—OPTION 1

HOWZITGOIN'

Time: about 5 minutes, depending on attendance
Supplies: pencils, prepared poster

Before kids arrive, draw a line on a poster. Place a 1 on the left end of the line, a 10 on the right, and a 5 in the middle. As kids arrive, ask them to pencil in their initials on the line.

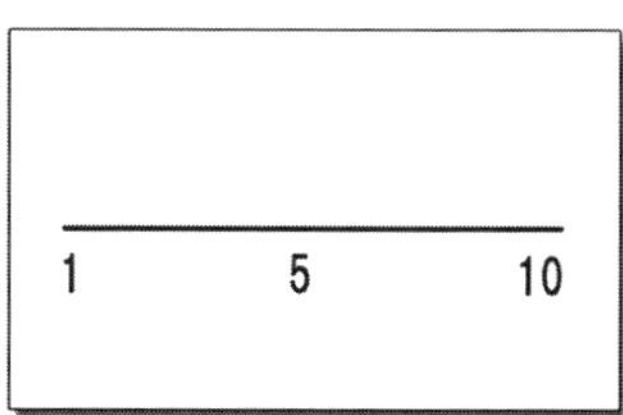

Say: **If this past week was so awful you wish you'd slept through it, place your initials by the 1. If it was a great week you wish you could repeat, put your initials by the 10. Place your initials anywhere on the line that shows how you feel about this past week—except exactly on the 5. That's because there's no such thing as a week that's exactly half good and half bad!**

After kids have signed in, give them 30 seconds each to explain why they placed their initials where they did. Be sure to include your own initials and explain your placement on the line. Kids will begin to express themselves more over time—and hearing their stories will help you adapt this lesson to make it relevant to your kids' lives.

OPENING ACTIVITY—OPTION 2

THE APPLE OF GOD'S EYE

Time: about 10 minutes
Supplies: 1 apple per child (and a few extra), paper towels, 1 bowl of water

Ask children to sit in a circle. Place a selection of apples in the middle of the circle.

Say: **Look at the apples, and then pick out one that reminds you of**

yourself for some reason. Maybe it's a bit bruised—and so are you. Maybe it has a dent, and you've always liked your dimples. Maybe it's big, and you're tall. For whatever reason, pick an apple.

After everyone has chosen an apple, invite them to use water and paper towels to polish up their apples.

Say: **Find a partner and introduce your apple. Explain why it reminds you of yourself. Then tell your friend about an area of your life where you shine—or an area where you're learning to do something well. Maybe you like music and you're learning to play guitar. Or you like math and you're learning how to do some hard math problems. Or you like helping in the kitchen and enjoy making cookies . . . that you'll bring with you next time!**

Give children time to talk. Then draw attention back to yourself. Say: **We're sort of like these apples. In some ways we shine. In other ways, we need a little polishing.**

In the story we'll explore today, we'll find a couple of people who did some shining. We'll also meet someone who could use a bit of polishing. And we'll discover an important truth: we should use our talents to serve God! Collect the apples.

Cool Story Game

Wrap—Unwrap

Time: 10 minutes or more, as desired

Supplies: 2 or 3 rubber bands per child, newspapers, 1 apple per child

Hand out the apples. Scatter the rubber bands and newspaper pages on the floor. Ask children to sit in a circle with their backs to the supplies, and to hold their apples in front of them.

Say: **In our Bible story we'll meet a couple of people who were given money to use in making more money. It's as if they were given a gift and had to figure out how to unwrap it to see the possibilities inside.**

I can't give you a bunch of money to invest, but I can give you the apple you're holding—and which you can't take a bite out of yet.

You'll unwrap your apples, so first you have to wrap them. Here's how you'll do it: First, hold your apple behind your back with both hands. When I tell you to move, scoot back and tear a piece of wrapping paper—that's the newspaper—to fit your apple. Then use rubber bands to hold the paper in place. And do all this with your hands behind your back. It's hard—but you can do it! Ready? (Have younger kids wrap their apples in front of themselves if they become too frustrated.)

Give children several minutes. Then invite them to show a partner how they did. Offer them the chance to adjust the wrapping so it's more secure and attractive.

Ask children to form pairs and discuss:

- ***What will eventually happen to your apple if it's not unwrapped?***
- ***How is an unused or uneaten apple a waste of food?***
- ***What happens to our talents if we never use them?***

Say: **It's unwrapping time! Take care of that task and enjoy an apple treat as we dive into a story about three servants!**

Cool BIBLE STORY

THREE. TWO. ONE . . . SERVE!

Time: about 15 minutes
Supplies: Bible

Form children into three groups: the Three-Talent Group, the Two-Talent Group, and the One-Talent Wonders. Not many children? A team can be as little as one child, and you can take on one of the roles yourself, if necessary (the One-Talent Wonders).

Say: **Here's a bit of background for this story Jesus told. In Jesus' day, a *talent* was a measure of money—and a lot of money. The man taking a trip wanted his trusted servants to manage his business and use his money to make a profit. It's as if I gave you $100 and asked you to do something with it to earn even more money while I was away awhile.**

Let's see what happened to the three servants. After we read from the Bible, you'll discuss answers to questions in your small groups.

Read aloud Matthew 25:14, 15. If one of your children is a skilled reader, ask that child to read passages aloud. Then ask:

- ***Why did the servants get different amounts of money?***

After kids share their thoughts with their groups, say: **The man who handed out money knew what his servants could do. The servants with more abilities received more coins. They would be able to do what he expected if they worked hard.**

Read aloud Matthew 25:16-18. Ask groups to discuss:

- ***Could you hide your money and still make more? Why not?***
- ***If I gave you money and you had to double it, how would you do that?***

Unless you have some young entrepreneurs in your group, it's unlikely they'll know how to answer. Suggest that they could start a business, making things to sell or buying stuff and reselling it. Challenge groups to brainstorm ways kids could create a business.

After exploring—and affirming—several ideas (lemonade stand, dog walking service, buying day-old donuts cheap and selling them at full price at a bus stop), continue reading aloud Matthew 25:19-29. Then ask:

- ***Who was most popular with the master? Why?***
- ***Why was the master unhappy with the One-Talent Wonder?***
- ***How is this like what happens in real life?***

Say: **To please God you don't have to be perfect. He already knows none of us is perfect—that's why Jesus had to come and die in our place. You need to have a heart for God—to want to please him. And you've got to give him your best so he can use it and use you too. The One-Talent Wonder didn't give his best. He didn't even try to please his master.**

As we pray, you'll consider a skill that God has given you. It's important that you do what the other servants in the story did: use that talent or skill for God. Let it grow as you serve him.

CLOSING PRAYER

TALENT SEARCH PRAYER

Time: about 10 minutes

Supplies: 1 sheet of paper and 1 pencil per child, 1 bowl

Give each child a sheet of paper and a pencil. Place a bowl on a tabletop or in another place where it's visible.

Say: **Ever heard of a talent search? It's when a show holds tryouts so talented people can come in and show their stuff. If they're picked, they get to go on stage or television and see if they can win a prize.**

We're going to have a talent search too—but we don't have to look hard. Why? Because all of you have at least one thing you can do to serve God. And you've already won the prize: you get to serve God!

On your paper write one skill or talent you have that you're willing to let God use. Maybe it's something you're really good at or just something you enjoy. What matters is that you're willing to let God use it. No one will see what you write except you and God.

Pause as children think and write. Ask them to fold their papers over one time. Invite children to place their folded papers in the bowl—but only if they're willing to let God use what they wrote down.

Close in prayer. Thank God for the ways he uses our gifts and talents to serve him.

AGE-ALERT TIPS

If you have **younger children** who find it too challenging to write about their gifts and talents, invite them to draw pictures of themselves using special talents they may have.

EXTRA-TIME ACTIVITY—OPTION 1

UNEXPECTED TALENTS #1: IMPERSONATIONS

Time: about 10 minutes
Supplies: paper and pencil (optional)

Think of this as a game of instant charades. Kids will take turns doing impersonations, or pantomimes, of animals and objects. The other children will have up to 30 seconds to identify what's being impersonated. Use the suggestions in the list below to get you started, and add more as desired. Tell kids that no words may be used, though it's fine to use sound effects.

If you wish (before kids arrive), write down each object or animal in the following list on a separate scrap of paper to distribute. Or you may simply whisper the name of an item to a child when it's his or her turn.

- Duck
- Goose
- Moose
- Hippo
- Hamster
- Kitten
- Giraffe
- Bunny
- Horse
- Fish
- Skunk
- Frog
- Hot air balloon
- Popcorn popping
- Teakettle
- Roller coaster
- Computer keyboard
- Traffic light
- Folded newspaper
- Lion tamer
- Flag in the breeze
- Camera
- Sea turtle
- Anteater

When your group has finished demonstrating both impersonation and guessing talents, have children sit in a circle and discuss:

- ***How could you use a talent for impersonation to serve God?***
- ***How might you use a gift of paying attention to people and knowing what they were trying to tell you to serve God?***
- ***What's a talent someone might have that just couldn't ever be used to serve God?***
- ***How might that talent be changed so it could be used to serve God?***

EXTRA-TIME ACTIVITY—OPTION 2

UNEXPECTED TALENTS #2: TIGHTROPE WALKING

Time: 5 minutes
Supplies: none

Explain to children that the invisible line between two points in the room is actually a tightrope strung between two high buildings. Ask them to take turns walking the tightrope, eyes closed, as you describe weather conditions and other things that are happening around the walker. Extra points for convincing movements!

As children walk, call out one or more of the following conditions: rain, high wind, slippery rope, a tornado passing by, a hurricane wave, an untied shoelace that must be tied again, a sudden need to use the restroom.

This simple activity can have hugely funny results as kids pinwheel from one point to the other.

At the end, have kids applaud each others' effort. Then say: **Great job! You have talents none of you even knew about before you walked into the room! As you grow up, you'll discover more talents that you have too. Remember that your talents are like gifts. So always unwrap those gifts to help others—and to serve God!**

EXTRA-TIME ACTIVITY—OPTION 3

INQUIRING MINDS WANT TO KNOW

Time: 5 minutes
Supplies: none

Gather kids in a circle. Ask: ***Some people have talents that never get used in church. Do those talents count as serving God? Why or why not?***

SESSION 7

The Story of the Rich Fool

The Point: Keep God first!
Scripture Connect: Luke 12:16-21

Supplies for all Session 7 activities options: pencils, prepared poster, at least 5 paper or foam cups per child, watch with a second hand, Bible, 1 hat, paper, 1 cooking spoon

The Basics for Leaders

A crowd had formed around Jesus, people pushing and elbowing to get near enough to hear. And a voice cried out from the crowd: "Teacher, please tell my brother to divide our father's estate with me!"

A practical request—but one easily settled by law and custom. Jesus saw something lurking beneath the request and that's what he addressed: greed. More specifically, how concern about wealth on earth gets in the way of being rich in a relationship with God.

Keeping God first is more than just a set of rules. It's more than doing the right thing at the right time. It's doing the right thing at the right time for the right reason. And that reason is a deepening love for God.

Through today's story you'll help children discover what a rich fool should have discovered: it's a good idea to keep God first!

OPENING ACTIVITY—OPTION 1

HOWZITGOIN'

Time: about 5 minutes, depending on attendance
Supplies: pencils, prepared poster

Before kids arrive, draw a line on a poster. Place a 1 on the left end of the line, a 10 on the right, and a 5 in the middle. As kids arrive, ask them to pencil in their initials on the line.

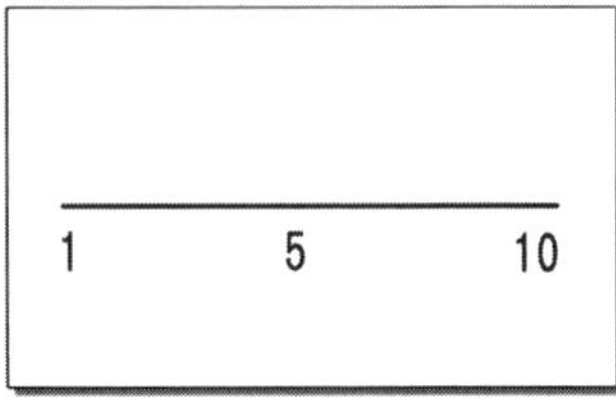

Say: **If this past week was so awful you wish you'd slept through it, place your initials by the 1. If it was a great week you wish you could repeat, put your initials by the 10. Place your initials anywhere on the line that shows how you feel about this past week—except exactly on the 5. That's because there's no such thing as a week that's exactly half good and half bad!**

After kids have signed in, give them 30 seconds each to explain why they placed their initials where they did. Be sure to include your own initials and explain your placement on the line. Kids will begin to express themselves more over time—and hearing their stories will help you adapt this lesson to make it relevant to your kids' lives.

OPENING ACTIVITY—OPTION 2

FIRST IN LINE

Time: about 10 minutes
Supplies: none

Have children face you, single file. Then ask them to line up again, but in alphabetical order of their first names. Have older kids help younger ones get in their correct places in line.

Applaud the effort, but tell children to move more quickly as they line up several more times. For each of the following rounds, ask kids to get lined up within 30 seconds.

Have children line up by height, exact age, alphabetical order of their middle names, distance to their homes from your meeting place, the number of buttons being worn, alphabetical order of their birthplace (city), or hair length. Keep lineups moving quickly—it's more fun!

After playing several rounds, say: **Most people love being first in line—and it was fun in this game too. But when it comes to putting someone else first in your life, who gets that spot? Is it you . . . someone else . . . or God?**

Today we'll dive into a story Jesus told about a rich fool and see what he learned about putting God first.

Cool Story Game

How High Can You Go?

Time: about 10 minutes

Supplies: at least 5 paper or foam cups per child, watch with a second hand

Form children into even-numbered teams. (You may need to join a team to keep the numbers even.) Give each team the same number of cups and this challenge: stack cups to make the tallest tower possible. Explain and demonstrate the following rules:

- **The first cup must be placed on the floor (or a table) right side up. The next cup is placed upside down over it. Continue this pattern to make a tall tower.**
- **Cups must be freestanding.**
- **Team members must take turns placing cups on the tower.**
- **Whichever tower is highest at the final signal wins—and I won't announce how long you have to work in each of three rounds.**

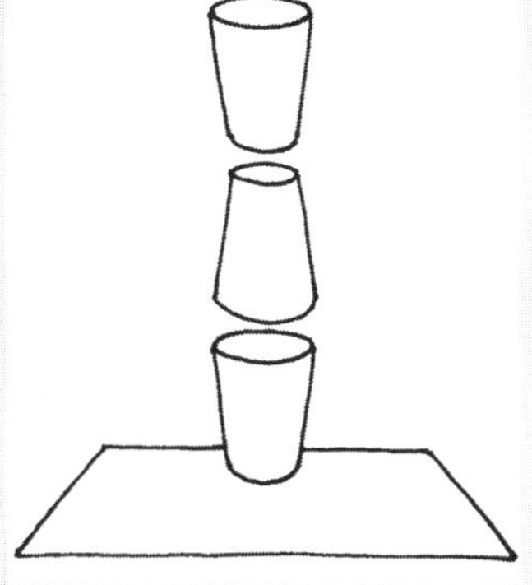

Say: **A winning tower might be just one cup high, depending on when time is called. Or it might be ten cups high or more. And if your tower of eight cups is steady, maybe it's not a good idea to get greedy and go for a tower of ten cups—even if you have time to keep building. It's up to you. Ready? Go!**

Vary the times of each round. Suggested: 25 seconds for the first round, 47 seconds for the second, and 30 seconds for the third round.

Collect the cups and gather children in a circle. Discuss as a group:

- ***What encouraged you to keep adding cups? to stop adding them?***
- ***How did it feel when your tower fell?***
- ***How was this activity like people always wanting more?***
- ***In what way, if any, did greed play a part in this activity?***

Say: **Let's meet a man Jesus described in a story. He was like many people we know—he wanted more and more. He had a lot of trust in his money, but he ran into a snag.**

Cool BIBLE STORY

LAST INTERVIEW

Time: about 15 minutes
Supplies: Bible, 1 hat, 1 pencil

Gather children in a circle. Say: **Good news! A newspaper reporter is coming any minute to interview you for an article. Word has gotten out about how you're going to put up some new barns on your farm. Wait . . . you don't know anything about this, do you?**

Explain to kids that they'll play the part of a successful farmer, and you'll play the part of a newspaper reporter. They've got to become very familiar with the details, so read aloud Luke 12:16-19. Explain that any details they're asked about will have to fit with the larger story—that they grow wheat and probably some other crops, and they're building bigger barns. In other words, they're rich! But other details? Those they can make up.

Pull on your reporter hat and pretend a pencil is a microphone. Then ask:

- ***How long have you been in farming?***
- ***Why do you think your fields have such large harvests?***
- ***How many people do you hire to work on your farm?***

- ***What crops do you grow?***
- ***How large will your new barns be? When will they be finished?***
- ***Now that you're rich, what will you do?***
- ***Were you surprised about the announcement?***

Your children won't know quite how to respond to the last question. You may hear, "What announcement?"

Say: **Oh, you thought I was from the *business page* of the paper. I'm not. I write the obituaries. I write about people who've just died. Or in your case, people who are about to die. I guess you didn't hear the rest of Jesus' story. Let's hear it now!**

Read aloud verses 20, 21.

Say: **So, Mr. Rich Farmer, how would you answer these questions?**

- ***What do you think your bigger barns will do for you now?***
- ***What matters more: your riches or your friendship with God?***
- ***Is it ever too late to put God first? Explain.***

Pull off your hat. Thank your kids for playing the part of the rich farmer. Then say: **Our farmer friend discovered—too late—that riches don't take the place of loving and serving God. You can't trust money to get to Heaven! For that you have to put God first!**

CLOSING PRAYER

GIVE-TO-GOD PRAYER

Time: about 5 minutes
Supplies: none

Gather kids and ask: **Is it OK to have stuff and to have money?** Give children time to respond.

Say: **Money isn't good or bad. It is just . . . money. What matters most is the *place* money has in your life and what you do with the money you have.**

Let's thank God for the money he's given to us and to our families.

And let's tell him that when it comes to money, we'll put God first.

Ask children to pray with their palms open and up, as a symbol of their willingness to give all they have to God. Ask children to briefly pray aloud, mentioning one thing they have that they consider valuable—and offering it to God. Close the prayer time by doing the same yourself.

EXTRA-TIME ACTIVITY—OPTION 1

INSTANT MILLIONAIRE—10 TIMES OVER!

Time: about 5 minutes

Supplies: 1 sheet of paper and 1 pencil per child

Woo-hoo! Every child in your group has just received $10 million from an unknown donor. But there's a catch: the money must be spent on themselves or others, or given away, in the next five minutes.

Give each child a sheet of paper and a pencil for taking notes. Then give them this challenge: **How will you get rid of your $10 million? Be ready to report back in five minutes!**

Ask children to report back to the larger group. Then ask:

- ***How many of you will need a bigger house to keep your stuff?***
- ***How did you decide where to give money?***
- ***If you could change your plan, how would you change it?***

Say: **How much is enough? How much is too much? The rich fool had too much—not because he had to build bigger barns, but because he quit putting God first. Instead, he put money first. Are you putting God first in your life—before anything or anyone else?**

AGE-ALERT TIPS

Both **young children** and **older kids** will enjoy finding pictures of what they could buy for others in magazines, newspapers, or old catalogs (if they're available). Consider pairing younger kids with older partners to help with the "spending."

EXTRA-TIME ACTIVITY—OPTION 2

YOUNG AND OLD

Time: about 5 minutes
Supplies: 1 cooking spoon

Ask children to sit in a circle on the floor, all within range of leaning forward and picking up the spoon. Explain that you're about to call out the name of an animal. Kids who know the correct name for the animal's young will grab for the spoon. For example, if you say "cat," the first person to grab for the spoon should say "kitten!" Whoever nabs the spoon first can offer a guess. If it's correct—great! If not, you'll replace the spoon and ask again. Adapt the game as necessary to give younger children an equal chance.

Here are pairings—the grown-up animal's name followed by the name of the animal when young.

- Chicken (chick)
- Alligator (hatchling)
- Kangaroo (joey)
- Bat (pup)
- Sea lion (pup)
- Deer (fawn)
- Frog (polliwog)
- Goose (gosling)

Say: **In nature the young come first—and then they turn into adults. It doesn't work the other way. In the kingdom of God, we have to put God first or things don't work either. It doesn't work any other way. Let's do what the rich man should have done: keep God first!**

EXTRA-TIME ACTIVITY—OPTION 3

INQUIRING MINDS WANT TO KNOW

Time: 5 minutes
Supplies: none

Gather kids in a circle. Ask: ***If you really put God first, what might change in your life?***

SESSION 8

The Story of the Two Builders

The Point: Obey Jesus.
Scripture Connect: Matthew 7:24-27

Supplies for all Session 8 activities options: pencils, prepared poster, 2 or more sofa cushions, popped popcorn, blankets (if needed), Bible, 1 cooking spoon

The Basics for Leaders

For much of his ministry, Jesus was the biggest show in town. Thousands of people would come to hear him teach. They hoped to see him heal a man with leprosy or feed an entire crowd with just a few fish sandwiches.

It's one thing to hear Jesus teach. It's another to take his teaching to heart—and obey him.

That's the heart of the story you'll share with children today—that when we obey Jesus, we build our lives on something solid and unmovable, something steady, something that won't shift or fall apart. Ever.

Help your kids discover that truth today: it's wise to obey Jesus!

OPENING ACTIVITY—OPTION 1

HOWZITGOIN'

Time: about 5 minutes, depending on attendance
Supplies: pencils, prepared poster

Before kids arrive, draw a line on a poster. Place a 1 on the left end of the line, a 10 on the right, and a 5 in the middle. As kids arrive, ask them to pencil in their initials on the line.

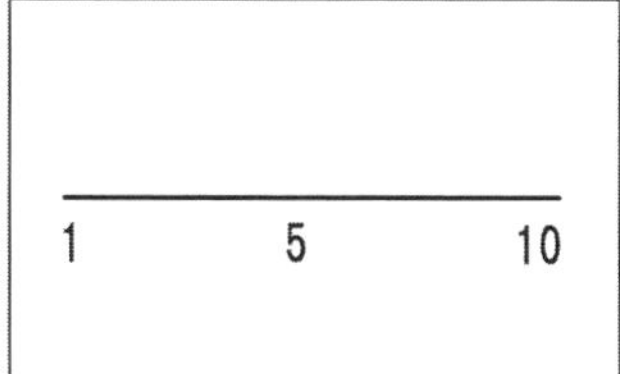

Say: **If this past week was so awful you wish you'd slept through it, place your initials by the 1. If it was a great week you wish you could repeat, put your initials by the 10. Place your initials anywhere on the line that shows how you feel about this past week—except exactly on the 5. That's because there's no such thing as a week that's exactly half good and half bad!**

After kids have signed in, give them 30 seconds each to explain why they placed their initials where they did. Be sure to include your own initials and explain your placement on the line. Kids will begin to express themselves more over time—and hearing their stories will help you adapt this lesson to make it relevant to your kids' lives.

OPENING ACTIVITY—OPTION 2

SOLID FOUNDATION

Time: about 10 minutes

Supplies: 2 or more sofa cushions

Ask children to remove their shoes and socks. Place cushions on the floor.

Say: **You're about to do something difficult: stand on these cushions. Trust me—it's harder than it looks.**

Form children into two teams and then have a child from Team One stand on the cushions—opposite a child on Team Two who is standing on the floor.

Ask both children to do the following:

- Stand on both feet, arms outstretched to the side, eyes open.
- The same as step one, but on one foot only.
- The same as step two, but with eyes closed.
- The same as step three, but with arms at the child's sides.

Children on the cushions will start wobbling at step three, so stand close so you can spot them. If you have lots of children (and lots of cushions), have more than one child stand on cushions at a time, but make sure you have adequate, responsible spotters.

After kids have finished, have teams switch locations so everyone can feel what it's like to follow the instructions while standing on the cushions and the floor. Then discuss:

- ***How tempted were you to open your eyes? Did you open your eyes?***
- ***Why couldn't you stand firm?***
- ***How would it have changed things if you'd been able to open your eyes?***

Say: **Your brain didn't have the information you needed to keep your balance. That's why you wanted to open your eyes.**

When you don't have a steady, solid foundation, it's easy to fall over. When you don't have the information you need to stay steady, it's easy to tip in the wrong direction.

That's true about your life too. Today we'll dive into a story Jesus told about two builders who chose to place houses on two very different foundations!

Cool Story Game

Blow Hard

Time: about 10 minutes

Supplies: 1 popped kernel of popcorn per child, blankets (if needed)

Before children arrive, identify at least two different surfaces for the Blow Hard game. Look for varying amounts of friction such as a hardwood or tile floor and a carpeted floor. No way to leave your room? Use the floor you have and place several thick blankets on it to provide more friction.

Give each child a kernel of popped popcorn. Ask children to put their kernels in a line on the floor and about 8 feet from a wall. Have children propel their popcorn forward by blowing on it. The goal: to reach the wall first.

Give a three, two, one countdown, and then start the race. Step quickly to the wall to be the line judge for the big finish.

Repeat the race several times on different surfaces.

Applaud all efforts, collect the kernels, and say: **Great job! Maybe you noticed that how hard you had to work depended on how smooth the surface was where you raced.**

The foundation you pick makes a difference! That's what two builders discovered in a story Jesus told. Let's dive into it and see what happened to them.

BEACH HOUSE BONANZA

Time: about 15 minutes
Supplies: Bible

Gather children in a circle and have them number off one, two, one, two around the circle. You'll be the reader, so you won't take a number.

Say: **Congratulations! Each of you has just won a new beach house—one that you can have built any way you want! Turn to a partner and tell that person what you want to be a part of your new home. For instance, I want a full-size basketball court just off my bedroom** (substitute any great big dream or wish).

Allow several moments to share. Then ask kids to report back how they'd create their new houses. Applaud their ideas.

Say: **Here's the thing: you number one builders will have your house built on a hill overlooking the beach. It has a nice view and is just a five-minute walk down to the water. The hill is solid rock, so it's a sturdy foundation.**

The number two builders will have your house built right on the beach. If you were any closer to the water, you could fish right off your porch. Your beach house is built on soft sand. So when the wind and waves are high, the sand under your house moves around.

Let's see how that turns out for you as we consider a story Jesus told about two builders. One builder put a new house on rock—that's you number one builders. The other builder put his house on sand—that's you number two builders.

As I read, I'd like you all to make sound effects. Ready?

Read aloud Matthew 7:24-27. Encourage kids to add sound effects at these points:

- verse 25: rain
- verse 25: floodwaters rushing in
- verse 25: winds howling
- verse 27: rain
- verse 27: floodwaters rising
- verse 27: winds howling

Say: **Number one builders, how did your house do?** Pause for answers. **You're rock solid because you're built on rock—a firm foundation.**

Number two builders, how did your house do? Encourage these kids to fall over onto the floor, like their house fell over.

Ask kids to form pairs and discuss:

- ***What made one builder foolish and the other wise?***
- ***How can you tell if your life is built on rock or sand?***
- ***What's a storm—a tough thing—that's happened to you? Did knowing Jesus help you stay strong? If so, how?***

Say: **When we listen to Jesus and follow his teaching, he helps us make good decisions. We build our lives on a solid foundation. It's wise to obey Jesus!**

CLOSING PRAYER

FIRM FOUNDATIONS PRAYER

Time: about 5 minutes
Supplies: none

Ask children to start their prayer time on all fours—with both knees and hands on the floor. Explain that you'll ask them to change positions three times as you pray together.

Pray: **God, thank you for the firm foundation of your love and your Word. We want to be wise in where we build our lives—so we ask your help building our lives on you.**

Ask children to raise one arm so they're touching the floor with just one hand and both of their knees.

Pray: **We pray for those who aren't strong or sturdy in their faith. Sometimes it's us, God. Help us to know and love you more.**

Ask children to shift so they're touching the floor with just one hand and one knee.

Pray: **We pray for those times we forget to obey you, God. When that happens we lose our firm foundation. Forgive us for those times.**

Ask children to shift so they're touching the floor with just one hand or knee. (Of course, they will probably topple over.)

Pray: **We know that, when we don't obey, we lose our firm foundation, God, and fall without you.** Have kids kneel or stand in a steady position. Say: **Thank you for loving us even then, and for giving us the chance to come back to you through love and obedience. Amen.**

Ask children to sit on the floor and discuss:

- ***When was it easiest to pray: when you had a firm foundation or a shaky one? Why?***

After your discussion, ask children to offer one-sentence prayers thanking God for being a solid rock they can count on.

EXTRA-TIME ACTIVITY—OPTION 1

DO AS I SAY. NOT AS I DO

Time: about 10 minutes
Supplies: none

This will take some practice on your part—but it's worth the effort.

In this version of Simon Says, you say one thing but do another. For instance, you may say "touch your knee" while you touch your elbow.

Tell children to obey what you say, not what you actually do. Then lead kids in a fast-paced game of Simon Says that involves various actions, such as: standing on one foot, touching various body parts, leaning in different directions, or jumping.

When you've finished, expect kids to be thoroughly confused. Discuss:

- ***What made it hard to obey in this game?***
- ***How do you feel when someone says to do something that he or she doesn't do? Why?***

Say: **Good news! Jesus asks us to obey him and to do what he wants. And he shows us how to be obedient. He did exactly what God wanted him to do. We can obey Jesus!**

EXTRA-TIME ACTIVITY—OPTION 2

FOUNDATION QUIZ

Time: about 10 minutes
Supplies: 1 cooking spoon

Place a cooking spoon on the floor and have children sit in a circle within range of leaning forward and picking up the spoon.

Explain that you'll call out the name of a famous building or landmark. You want to know where the "foundation" for that building or landmark is—the city or the country where the landmark is found. Whoever knows the answer can grab the spoon and offer a guess. If it's correct, go to the next item on your list! If not, replace the spoon and ask again.

If you have at least two older and two younger children, pair them up to make the contest more equal.

Here are buildings or landmarks—and the answers!

AGE-ALERT TIPS

If you have **younger children,** use these easier landmarks:

- Their own houses
- Their schools
- A park they enjoy

- The Eiffel Tower (Paris, France)
- The Great Pyramids (Egypt)
- The London Bridge (Lake Havasu City, Arizona)
- Lincoln's Tomb (Springfield, Illinois)
- Great Wall of China (China)
- The Taj Mahal (Agra, India)

Say: **These buildings and landmarks have firm foundations—so they've lasted. Is your foundation as solid because it's based on your friendship with God through Jesus?**

We build a solid foundation for our lives when we love and obey Jesus. That's a rock-solid foundation that lasts forever!

EXTRA-TIME ACTIVITY—OPTION 3

INQUIRING MINDS WANT TO KNOW

Time: 5 minutes

Supplies: none

Gather kids in a circle. Ask: ***What rules at home do you find hardest to obey? Why? What do you think Jesus wants you to do about that?***

SESSION 9

The Story of the Vine & Branches

The Point: Stay connected to Jesus.
Scripture Connect: John 15:1, 4, 5

Supplies for all Session 9 activities options: pencils, prepared poster, tape measure, Bible, shoes the kids are wearing

The Basics for Leaders

During Jesus' time on earth, most people who heard him speak worked in agriculture. Even people who lived in cities were used to seeing grapevines dot the landscape, each vine carefully tended so it produced branches heavy with grapes at harvesttime.

So nobody missed Jesus' point: if you want grapes to grow on a branch, the worst thing you can do is remove that branch from the grapevine.

The grapevine carries life-giving nourishment to the branch. It's what keeps branches from turning into kindling for the next cooking fire.

What was challenging for his audience to grasp was the meaning of Jesus' words: that when we remain in Jesus—when we stay connected to him—he can do great things through us. You'll help your kids discover the truth in Jesus' words: they can stay connected to Jesus!

OPENING ACTIVITY—OPTION 1

HOWZITGOIN'

Time: about 5 minutes, depending on attendance
Supplies: pencils, prepared poster

Before kids arrive, draw a line on a poster. Place a 1 on the left end of the line, a 10 on the right, and a 5 in the middle. As kids arrive, ask them to pencil in their initials on the line.

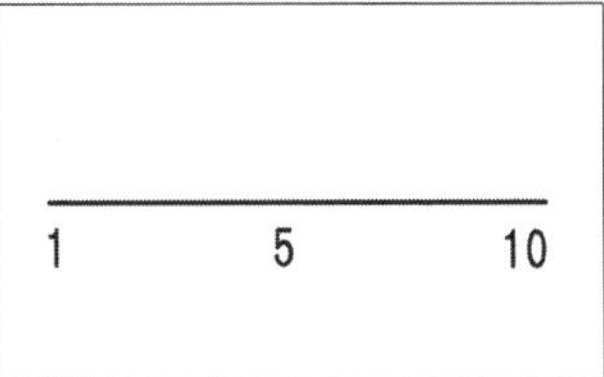

Say: **If this past week was so awful you wish you'd slept through it, place your initials by the 1. If it was a great week you wish you could repeat, put your initials by the 10. Place your initials anywhere on the line that shows how you feel about this past week—except exactly on the 5. That's because there's no such thing as a week that's exactly half good and half bad!**

After kids have signed in, give them 30 seconds each to explain why they placed their initials where they did. Be sure to include your own initials and explain your placement on the line. Kids will begin to express themselves more over time—and hearing their stories will help you adapt this lesson to make it relevant to your kids' lives.

OPENING ACTIVITY—OPTION 2

CONNECTION DETECTION

Time: about 10 minutes
Supplies: none

Form children into pairs and sit each pair on the floor, partners facing each other.

Say: **Time to see how closely we're connected together. When I give the signal, see how quickly you can find three things you have in common. When you've got three, call out, "Connected!"**

And dig a bit. It doesn't count that you both have noses! Look for things like both your birthdays are in the spring or you each have a middle name with five letters. Start now. Uneven number of kids? Jump in yourself to form a pair.

After kids complete the first round, play three more rounds, looking for four, five, and six new connections.

This game becomes increasingly difficult as the easy connections are covered. After kids either struggle through the third round or abandon hope, say: **Let's change the rules a bit to see if it helps. This last round you only need to find two connections—but you have to sit back-to-back with your partner. Scoot into that position now.**

After kids move, continue with this instruction: **Oh, and you can't talk either. Ready? Go!** It won't take long for kids to realize they're stuck and to give up. Have kids gather in a large circle, facing in, for a discussion. Ask:

- ***What was easy or hard about this connection challenge?***
- ***What would have helped you succeed during the last round?***

Say: **The results I wanted—for you to find things you have in common with your partner—couldn't happen unless you were connected! It didn't help when I cut you off from the only source of information you had! Today we'll dive into a story Jesus told about staying connected. We'll discover that when we stay connected to Jesus, great things can happen.**

Cool Story Game

Get Connected!
Time: about 10 minutes
Supplies: tape measure

Ask children to stand against one wall. Instruct them to work together to make a single chain reaching as far as possible by connecting themselves and anything they brought with them. They can use belts, shoelaces, or strings of beads. So long as the chain has items connected—it counts!

Give kids several minutes to make their chain. Measure it with a tape measure and report the result. Applaud your kids' creativity and willingness to work together.

As kids replace their belts and shoelaces, ask them to discuss:

- ***How long a chain do you think you could have made on your own?***
- ***How was our working together helpful in making a longer chain?***

Say: **When we stayed connected, we could do more. That's something the people listening to Jesus discovered when they heard him share a story about a vine and a branch. Let's dig into that story and see what we can learn!**

Cool BIBLE STORY

FRUIT AND FIREWOOD

Time: about 20 minutes
Supplies: Bible

Gather children in a circle, seated close enough to hold hands when you ask them to do so. Say: **When Jesus was on earth, there were lots of vineyards in the area where he lived. People who heard Jesus speak knew how to care for a grapevine so it would produce a healthy harvest.**

One thing people did very carefully was to cut branches from the vine. Prune too much and there were no branches left to produce grapes. Prune too little and the grapes were small. But this was always true: once you cut a branch from the vine, that branch couldn't produce fruit! I'll read aloud a story Jesus shared about a grapevine. It's not much of a story—it's more a picture Jesus wanted his listeners to see and explore. So that's what we'll do!

Tell kids you'll be the gardener and they'll represent the branches—except for the last child in line. That child will represent the fruit. See the diagram on the next page for positioning: G (gardener), F (fruit), and X (branches).

Arrange your Bible so you can easily read aloud using just one hand to hold the Bible on your lap. With your other hand, hold the hand of the child next to you (the child playing the branch, not the fruit). Ask children to form a "vine" by holding the hands of kids next to them. Only you (the gardener) and the child playing the fruit will each have a free hand.

Say: **When your hand is squeezed, "pass along" the squeeze as quickly as possible to the next person in line. When the child playing the fruit feels his or her hand squeezed, that child will call out, "Fruit!"**

After everyone's connected, read aloud John 15:1, 4, 5. Squeeze a hand where indicated and wait until "Fruit!" is called each time:

"I am the true grapevine, (squeeze) **and my Father is the gardener."** (squeeze)

"Remain in me, and I will remain in you. (squeeze) **For a branch cannot produce fruit** (squeeze) **if it is severed from the vine, and you cannot be fruitful unless you remain in me.** (squeeze)

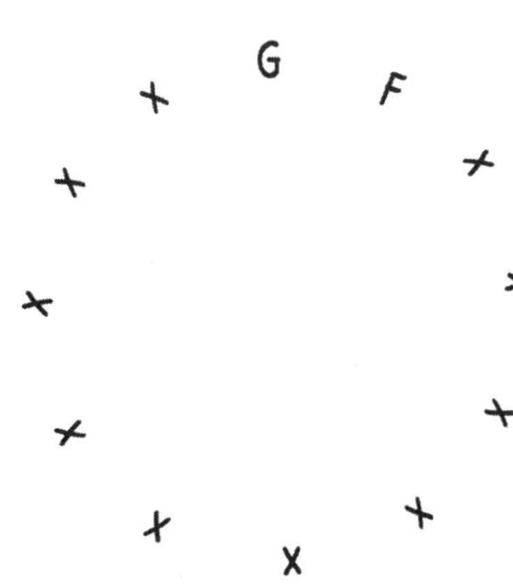

"Yes, I am the vine; (squeeze) **you are the branches. Those who remain in me, and I in them, will produce much fruit.** (squeeze) **For apart from me you can do nothing."** (squeeze)

Ask children to release their hands but stay in a circle. Discuss:

- ***What would have happened had someone dropped out of our vine?***
- ***What kinds of good fruit do you think Jesus is looking to find in his followers?***
- ***What kind of good fruit is growing in you? How do you know?***

Say: **Jesus is clear: when we stay connected to him and let him lead us, great things happen. But when we try to go it on our own—it's not so great. Let's thank Jesus that we can stay connected to him and for the way he helps us bear good fruit!**

CLOSING PRAYER

HANDS-ON PRAYER

Time: about 3 minutes

Supplies: none

Ask children to join you in a circle. Say: **If you believe in Jesus and have him as a friend, you're a branch in this story. You're connected to Jesus.**

He wants to give you strength to bear fruit and to be strong and helpful in his kingdom. Let's thank Jesus for connecting to us.

First, please place your hands down at your sides, pointed toward the floor, and join me as I pray. Jesus, thank you for rooting us in you—for letting us grow deep in our faith—for giving us a solid foundation in our lives. Thank you for your love.

Now please hold your hands up. (pause) **Jesus, we praise you. Only you could do what you've done—create a way for us to come to God through you. We honor you as our Savior.**

Now please join hands. (pause) **Jesus, thank you for letting us be connected to each other. Thank you for the strength that comes with serving you together. Thank you for our friends. Amen.**

EXTRA-TIME ACTIVITY—OPTION 1

TIDY TIE

Time: about 10 minutes
Supplies: shoes the kids are wearing

This object talk is best suited for older kids who are able to quickly lace and unlace their shoelaces. Have a child wearing slip-on shoes or sandals? No problem! Have that child help another child wearing lace-ups.

Ask children to remove their shoes. Say: **When I think of connections, I think of shoelaces. They not only connect to the shoes, but they keep your shoes connected to your feet.** Instruct children to put their shoes on and lace them in reverse order so that the laces tie at their toes instead of their ankles. Discuss:

- ***How are our shoelaces like a vine?***
- ***Why is it a good idea to stay connected to Jesus?***

When they're finished lacing up their shoes, ask children to leave them that way and see how long it takes their parents to notice the difference!

EXTRA-TIME ACTIVITY—OPTION 2

STICKING TOGETHER

Time: about 10 minutes
Supplies: shoes the kids are wearing

Ask children to remove their shoes. Place your guys with guys and girls with girls for this game, with each same-sex group forming a row against one wall. Within each row wedge a shoe between the elbows of every two children so the only way they can keep the shoes from falling is to press their elbows together tightly.

The goal is for each row to move together to the opposite wall without losing their shoes. If a shoe is lost, stop the line and replace the shoe before continuing.

AGE-ALERT TIPS

For **young children**, this activity can be a challenge. Consider skipping it if you have mostly younger kids, unless you have several volunteers help them accomplish the task.

At the end of the game, ask each team to discuss:

- ***What made it easy to stay connected? hard to stay connected?***
- ***What makes it easy or hard to stay connected with God?***

EXTRA-TIME ACTIVITY—OPTION 3

INQUIRING MINDS WANT TO KNOW

Time: 5 minutes
Supplies: none

Gather kids in a circle. Ask: ***Why do you think someone who knows Jesus would choose to not stay connected to him?***

SESSION 10

The Story of the Mean Servant

The Point: We can forgive others.
Scripture Connect: Matthew 18:21-35

Supplies for all Session 10 activities options: pencils; prepared poster; paper lunch sacks; markers; yarn, glitter, glue, felt (optional); Bible; dish towel; watch with a second hand; baking pan; variety of 30 or more objects from the junk drawer (buttons, nuts, bolts, nails, coins, beads); paper; 1 shoe

The Basics for Leaders

How many times do we need to forgive someone? *How many times?*

Seventy times seven—that was Jesus' reply.

That wasn't a literal answer. We know that 490 times isn't the cutoff point for grace. Jesus was making the point that forgiveness needs to be available until it's no longer sought or needed.

But there's another message in this story: forgiveness is a two-way street. Yes, we receive it from God through Jesus. But we're also expected to be just as forgiving to others.

In this session you'll help kids discover that the forgiveness they receive from God isn't just for them. God wants to empower us to be equally forgiving, to pass along what we've received. With his help, we can forgive others!

OPENING ACTIVITY—OPTION 1

HOWZITGOIN'

Time: about 5 minutes, depending on attendance
Supplies: pencils, prepared poster

Before kids arrive, draw a line on a poster. Place a 1 on the left end of the line, a 10 on the right, and a 5 in the middle. As kids arrive, ask them to pencil in their initials on the line.

Say: **If this past week was so awful you wish you'd slept through it, place your initials by the 1. If it was a great week you wish you could repeat, put your initials by the 10. Place your initials anywhere on the line that shows how you feel about this past week—except exactly on the 5. That's because there's no such thing as a week that's exactly half good and half bad!**

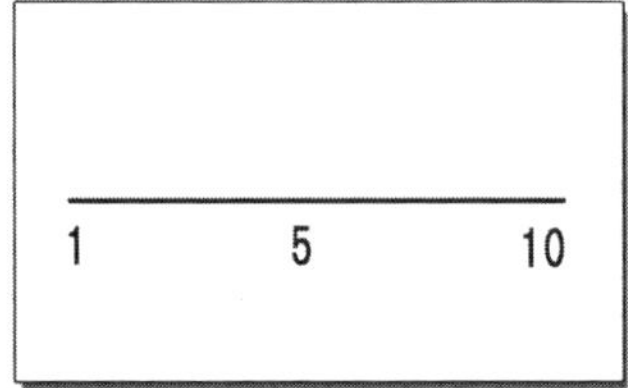

After kids have signed in, give them 30 seconds each to explain why they placed their initials where they did. Be sure to include your own initials and explain your placement on the line. Kids will begin to express themselves more over time—and hearing their stories will help you adapt this lesson to make it relevant to your kids' lives.

OPENING ACTIVITY—OPTION 2

STORY SACKS

Time: 10 minutes

Supplies: paper lunch sacks; markers; yarn, glitter, glue, felt (optional)

Kids will use these puppets later, so be sure everyone makes one. Before the activity, you may wish to make a puppet as a sample. Also refer to the illustration.

Ask kids to sit in a circle on the floor, and join them. Give each child a sack. Provide markers.

Say: **Today we'll dive into a story Jesus told about a man who got into big trouble. He owed lots of money! You're going to play a part in the story, so you each need to create a sack puppet that looks like you.**

If children aren't sure where to start, show them the illustration or your sample, if you made one. (If you're feeling especially crafty and have extra time, provide the optional supplies so kids can make more elaborate puppets.) Tell children they should keep their work hidden for now. They have just five minutes to create their masterpieces. Give a two- and one-minute countdown.

Once children have finished, collect the puppets and place them behind you, as you remain seated with the children on the floor.

Say: **Now let's see how much these puppets look like their creators. I'll show one puppet at a time. See if you can guess who it is.**

After the guessing is finished, say: **Great job!** Set the puppets aside.

Say: **Today we'll talk about forgiveness—about being forgiven by God and about forgiving others who do things to us. They're connected! God forgives us—so let's forgive others.**

Cool Story Game

Gone and Forgotten

Time: about 10 minutes

Supplies: Bible, dish towel, watch with a second hand, baking pan, variety of 30 or more objects from the junk drawer (buttons, nuts, bolts, nails, coins, beads)

Place the 30 objects in the pan, and cover them with the dish towel.

Gather children around the pan. Remove the towel and tell kids to look at the items in the pan and memorize them—in 30 seconds.

Then pick up the pan and turn your back on the kids. Remove one item—without letting them see it—and hide it in a pocket or somewhere else.

Rearrange the remaining items. Turn back to the children, and let them guess which item you removed. No hints!

Play several rounds. Then reveal and replace the missing items. Ask:

- ***What made it easy or difficult to remember all the items?***
- ***When have you forgotten something you needed to remember? What happened as a result?***
- ***What's something you think you'd like to forget?***

Say: **Our memories can play tricks on us. Things we want to remember, we sometimes forget. Things we'd rather forget, we sometimes remember. But here's something that's true: everybody forgets things . . . including God. That's right: God sometimes forgets things.**

Read aloud Hebrews 10:17.

Continue: **Once God forgives us for something, he chooses not to recall it, not to not bring it up again. And here's where things get hard: God wants us to forgive people in just the same way.**

Read aloud Luke 11:1-4a.

Say: **Notice the "forgive us as we forgive others" line. That means us. *We* are to forgive others as we want Jesus to forgive us. God forgives us—let's forgive others!**

Cool BIBLE STORY

THE NOT-SO-SMART SERVANT

Time: 15 minutes

Supplies: Bible, sack puppets from Opening Activity—Option 2

Assign the following roles to individual kids: king, king's servant, the servant's wife and children, and a second servant. (If you have more kids than roles, let them be extra children in the first servant's family.)

Say: **As I read aloud the story Jesus told, use your puppets to act out what happened to your characters. Feel free to move about. If your puppet is supposed to be afraid, shake in fear. If you're supposed to attack another character, gently go after that puppet. Your puppet has to do the acting—you're just along for the ride. And though there's no talking, please whimper, snort, or provide other sound effects as you wish.**

Read aloud Matthew 18:21-35, pausing often for the puppets to act out their roles.

> **AGE-ALERT TIPS**
>
> **Younger children** will need help in knowing when their puppet characters are to respond and may need a lot of guidance as to what their puppets can act out. Consider pairing younger kids with older ones who can help cue them in!

When you're done, have puppets take a bow. Collect them to send home later. Ask children to each sit facing a partner and discuss:

- ***What's the lesson about forgiveness that Jesus is trying to teach?***
- ***If Jesus is serious about that message, what does that mean to me?***

After kids finish talking, have them circle up with you. Ask what kids think the moral of the story is. Are they on target? Congratulate the children. Are they off target? Gently redirect your children.

Say: **Forgiveness is a two-way thing. Yes, God will forgive us if we ask. But we're expected to be just as forgiving. In that way we begin to show other people what God is like. God is forgiving—let's be forgiving too!**

CLOSING PRAYER

CONFESSION IS GOOD FOR THE SOUL

Time: 7 minutes
Supplies: none

Read 1 John 1:8, 9 aloud. Say: **God forgives, but he wants something from us when he forgives: he wants us to agree with him that what we**

did is wrong. That's called "confession." It's agreeing with God that the wrong thing we did is wrong.

We're going to confess to God and trust him to keep his word about forgiving us. We won't confess out loud here—though it's OK to do that sometimes. For now, please confess in your head and heart. I'll lead us.

Ask children to bow their heads and close their eyes. Tell them that they can add their own silent prayers in the pauses.

Pray: **Dear God, we trust that you keep your promises. We trust that if we confess, you will be faithful and just to forgive us our sins and to cleanse us from all wickedness.**

Please hear us as we tell you about thoughts we have that don't honor you. This includes our thoughts about people (pause) **and our thoughts about the lives you've given us.** (pause) **It also includes our thoughts about you and how important we make you in our lives.** (pause)

Forgive us for things we've done and for things that nobody knows about except us—and you. (pause)

Forgive things we've said, including angry words (pause) **and unfair words.** (pause) **Forgive us for words that have harmed others** (pause) **and words that don't honor you.** (pause)

We confess that all these things are sin. They don't please you, and we want to please you. They don't show you love, and we want to love you. Help us be as forgiving of others. Bring to mind one person we need to forgive. (pause)

Thank you for your forgiveness. Amen.

EXTRA-TIME ACTIVITY—OPTION 1

YOU'VE GOT MAIL

Time: about 10 minutes

Supplies: 1 sheet of paper and 1 pencil per child

Ask kids to sit on the floor. Give each child a sheet of paper and pencil.

Say: **We all have at least one person we could ask forgiveness from. Who is your person? Is that person someone at home or at school?**

Think about it for a moment and pick a person . . . and a reason you need to ask for forgiveness.

Pause for a few moments so children have time to think.

Say: **Now you get the chance to apologize—at least to practice apologizing. In the next few minutes write a note asking the person to forgive you. And be specific—mention what you did or said that needs to be forgiven.**

If you'd rather draw your apology, make a "Please Forgive Me" card. Draw a frown on the cover and a smile on the inside or decorate your card in another way.

Help young children write: "I'm sorry . . . please forgive me" on the insides of their cards.

Explain that kids don't have to give their notes and cards to the people they've wronged. This is just practice. But suggest that if children want to act but don't want to deliver notes and cards, they can simply talk to the people they've wronged and ask for their forgiveness.

Allow time to write or draw. Then have children find partners and discuss:

- ***What's hard about asking for forgiveness?***
- ***What would be a good thing about asking for forgiveness?***
- ***How does forgiving someone bring us closer to God?***

EXTRA-TIME ACTIVITY—OPTION 2

GOT IT. GIVE IT

Time: about 5 minutes
Supplies: watch with a second hand, 1 shoe

Ask children to sit in a circle. Invite a child to provide one shoe, or use yours. Choose a child who counts well to be the Lap Master, and hand that child the shoe. That child's job is to keep track of the number of times a shoe makes it around the circle by calling out the lap number as the shoe passes him or her. One time around? One lap. Twice around? Two laps.

The game's goal is to make as many laps as possible in 60 seconds. Tell kids there are three rules:

1. **No throwing! The shoe must be passed.**
2. **If the shoe is dropped, the Lap Master subtracts one lap from the total and everyone must say, "It's forgiven."**
3. **If someone makes a poor pass—the shoe is fumbled or falls in a player's lap—the person receiving the shoe says, "It's forgiven." No lost lap!**

Play three rounds, trying to increase the number of laps each time. At any time you can call "reverse" and send the shoe in the opposite direction.

After playing, discuss as a group:

- ***How was this game like real life when someone needs forgiveness?***
- ***In what ways does forgiving others make life—or our game—more pleasant?***

Say: **When we ask God's forgiveness, he forgives us. He knows that forgiving us helps us be healthier, happier, and closer to him. And we can forgive others as God forgives us!**

EXTRA-TIME ACTIVITY—OPTION 3

INQUIRING MINDS WANT TO KNOW

Time: 5 minutes
Supplies: none

Gather kids in a circle. Ask: ***If God was only as forgiving of you as you are of others, how forgiven would you feel? Why? What can you do to change that?***

SESSION 11

The Story of the Wedding Feast

The Point: You're invited to God's party!
Scripture Connect: Luke 14:16-24

Supplies for all Session 11 activities options: pencils, prepared poster, paper, markers, masking tape, Bible, lots of newspapers

The Basics for Leaders

Jesus was a dinner guest at the house of an important leader when he noticed that some of the guests were pushing to sit in the more honored seats, the ones closer to the host.

Jesus said a few words about humility, and then he told this story.

At that time, like now, it was important to know how many people were coming to a dinner party. That determined how much food was prepared. In this story, people accept the invitation and then, for a variety of reasons, don't show up—even though they get a reminder. This was not only rude, but an actual insult.

The host invites people who don't normally get invitations to banquets: people who are poor, crippled, lame, and blind. They'll never be able to return the invitation, but the food is ready . . . the table set . . . so they're invited in.

Jesus' point is that even people who don't "qualify" get invitations to be with him. They just have to agree to come.

Those people, by the way, include us. We're invited to God's party!

Help your kids discover they're invited today, and encourage them to say "Yes!" to Jesus' invitation!

OPENING ACTIVITY—OPTION 1

HOWZITGOIN'

Time: about 5 minutes, depending on attendance
Supplies: pencils, prepared poster

Before kids arrive, draw a line on a poster. Place a 1 on the left end of the line, a 10 on the right, and a 5 in the middle. As kids arrive, ask them to pencil in their initials on the line.

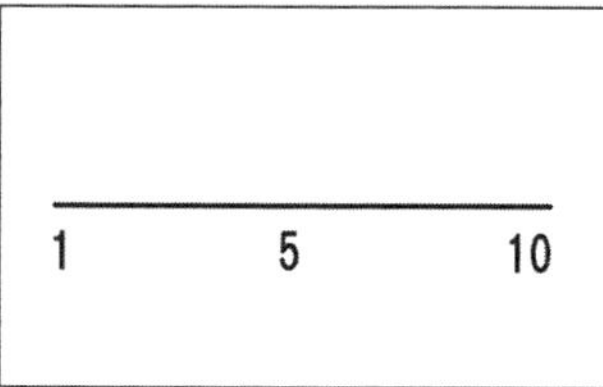

Say: **If this past week was so awful you wish you'd slept through it, place your initials by the 1. If it was a great week you wish you could repeat, put your initials by the 10. Place your initials anywhere on the line that shows how you feel about this past week—except exactly on the 5. That's because there's no such thing as a week that's exactly half good and half bad!**

After kids have signed in, give them 30 seconds each to explain why they placed their initials where they did. Be sure to include your own initials and explain your placement on the line. Kids will begin to express themselves more over time—and hearing their stories will help you adapt this lesson to make it relevant to your kids' lives.

OPENING ACTIVITY—OPTION 2

YOU'RE INVITED

Time: about 10 minutes
Supplies: 1 sheet of paper per child, markers

Invite children to tell you about parties they've attended and enjoyed. Have kids describe any costumes, decorations, or party favors. Describe any party games. Ask what made those parties so much fun.

Say: **Those sound like fun parties—but they aren't the best party ever. What would your best-ever party be like? Would you hold it at your house or on a yacht bobbing around in the ocean? Would you serve pizza or lobster? What would you and your guests do at your perfect party?**

Using paper and markers, create an invitation to the best party you can imagine. Write what guests would do at the party, how the guests should come dressed. List the food you'll serve. If you'll have a limo pick up guests, say so. Since money is no problem, be as bold as you can be! Go for it!

You'll have five minutes to create your invitation, and then we'll share what we wrote with others. Ready? Start inviting!

After five minutes, ask children to describe their parties to the larger group. Then as a group discuss:

- ***How would you feel if a friend agreed to come to your party—and then didn't show?***
- ***What would you say to your friend?***

Say: **Today we'll dig into a story Jesus told about people not showing up at a very special party. The food was ready, the invitations were accepted—but people didn't show up for that special party. What would the host do?**

Cool Story Game

Party Pooper

Time: 10 minutes or more, as desired
Supplies: masking tape

Place a length of masking tape on the floor in the center of the room. Have all the children stand on the tape, single file, facing you. (Make sure the tape line is only about as long as the line of kids.)

Say: **When people are planning parties there's always someone who says, "Nah—not me" to every activity suggestion. For instance, you**

might all say, "Let's go skydiving for Josh's birthday party. And I'd say, "Nah—not me."

Explain that in this game you'll suggest an activity. If a child would do it, he or she should step forward (in front of the line). If not, step backward behind the line. Either answer is OK—but if there's just one child behind the line, that person will be appointed the Designated Self-Confident Party Pooper. (Tell kids that it's an honor!) The Party Pooper may give everyone high fives before returning to the line.

After you name each activity and kids have stepped forward or backward, have them return to the masking tape line for the next activity choice. Move fast! Here are suggested activities to name. Add more, if desired:

- Go skydiving after one lesson
- Go snorkeling in a pool
- Snorkel in shark-infested seas
- Pop balloons by sitting on them
- Ride on a roller coaster
- Ride a roller coaster minus seat belts
- Go on a horse ride
- Go camping
- Go swimming in a pool
- Go swimming in a lake
- Dress up as superheroes
- Dress up as chickens
- Eat cake
- Eat chocolate
- Eat worms
- Eat chocolate-covered worms
- Plant a garden for yourself
- Plant a garden to feed families

Have children sit on the floor in a circle. Say: **At one time or another, we're all party poopers. But imagine throwing a party and everyone is a party pooper—so much so that they don't even show up!**

Let's see what happened when a man throwing a wedding party had that happen to him.

Cool BIBLE STORY

PARTY PREP ON A DIME

Time: about 20 minutes

Supplies: Bible, masking tape, lots of newspapers

Before children arrive, create a rectangle on the floor using masking tape. Make it the size of a generous dining room table. Place the newspapers outside the rectangle.

Tell children they have just eight minutes to get ready for a party—a formal party with four guests—and they have only the newspapers to create both place settings and decorations. They'll place what they create on the masking tape table you've outlined on the floor

Making place mats will be easy. Tearing out plates and platters—that will be tougher. Utensils will be a major challenge. And decorations and centerpieces? Good luck.

Spend a few quick moments brainstorming together who will do what, and then get busy—time is short!

After the eight frantic minutes, gather kids where they can admire their handiwork. Compliment them—they deserve it! Say: **Bad news: our four guests will be a little late. We sent out invitations, and they responded that they'd come on time—promised they'd come. We even reminded them earlier about coming.**

By late I mean: our guests aren't coming. At all. Ever. They all found something more important to do. Ask:

- ***How would you feel—after preparing a party and a feast—if your guests simply chose not to come?***

Say: **Have a seat around our table here, and as you enjoy an imaginary feast, I'll share with you a story Jesus shared with an audience.**

Read aloud Luke 14:16-24. Then discuss as a group:

- ***How do you think the master felt about the people he'd invited?***
- ***What do you think of the master's solution to finding guests?***

- ***Where do you think we fit into the story?***

Say: **When it comes to joining the kingdom of God, we're definitely latecomers. The Jews were God's chosen people, but after many of them refused to walk faithfully with God and with Jesus, non-Jews were invited too. Most of us aren't Jewish, so we're like those poor people who got to come to the feast too. Good news for us!**

But here's the truth: Jesus died for everyone—Jews and non-Jews alike. We're invited to God's party. All we have to do is say "yes" and go!

CLOSING PRAYER

RESPONDING TO GOD'S INVITATION

Time: about 5 minutes
Supplies: none

Ask children to stand in a circle, facing out. Tell them to close their eyes and keep their eyes closed until you say the "amen."

Say: **It's great that we've been invited to God's party, to come to him through his Son, Jesus. The party is our friendship with God, and it goes forever. It starts here, but one day we'll be with God in Heaven forever. The party never ends! But if we don't accept the invitation, it doesn't matter much. So we're now going to have a chance to say "yes."**

As I pray, please pray along with me. Talk to God about how you feel. At one point I'll invite you to turn around and face into the circle as a way of saying "yes" to God. Keep your eyes closed so you can't see how anyone else answers. What matters is whether you say "yes" to God—whether you accept his invitation to his party.

AGE-ALERT TIPS

For **younger** and **older children:** This prayer activity gives you insight into the spiritual life of any child. Who says "yes" and who doesn't respond? Pray accordingly. Then quietly follow up later with nonresponsive children to see if they want to talk further.

Pray: **Dear God, you're good. Every day, every moment, you're loving. We know you invite us to be your friends because you love us.**

Let's pause and thank God for his love. How has God shown love to you? Pray out loud or silently. I'll continue in a few moments. (pause)

Inviting us to be with you is a forever thing, God. You'll be our friend now—and forever in Heaven. Thank you for inviting us to be with you. (pause) **God, thank you for your invitation. You know us by name. You invite us by name.**

If you'd like to say "yes" to being God's friend, turn around in the circle. Keep your eyes closed. (pause)

Dear God, thank you for your invitation. We trust you and we say "yes," knowing that we can trust you forever. Amen.

EXTRA-TIME ACTIVITY—OPTION 1

PARTY FEET

Time: about 5 minutes
Supplies: none

Ask kids to line up against one wall. The goal: reach the opposite wall first. But—here's the catch—the only way to take a step forward is to first call out a type of party or a theme for a party. A second rule: you can't use a theme or type of party that's been called out by anyone else.

Ask children to take steps in rotation, one at a time, and allow just five seconds between answers. If a child can't think of a theme, that child loses a turn or you can help with an answer (great chance to show grace!).

Some unlikely-to-be-called party types and themes to pull out in a pinch: bachelorette, bachelor, luau, 99th birthday, coffee, Italian cuisine, gymnastics, Navy, World Day of Prayer, Australia Day (Australia), the Queen's Birthday (UK), Boxing Day, National Unity Day (Italy), Fisherman's Day (Marshall Islands), King Harald V's Birthday (Norway), Confederation Day.

When you've finished playing, read aloud John 3:16,17. Then ask:

- ***What would you say to a Live Forever with God party?***
- ***What would you give for an invitation to that party?***

EXTRA-TIME ACTIVITY—OPTION 2

MY NEW FAVORITE DESSERT!

Time: 10 minutes
Supplies: 1 sheet of paper and 1 pencil per child

Hold onto this list of ways to prepare or serve food: baked, boiled, braised, broiled, grilled, fried, frozen, poached, steamed, toasted, and raw.

Ask one or more children to write a list of at least ten ice cream flavors—the weirder, the better. Vanilla and chocolate will get a mention, but so should mangled mango or ketchup tofu.

Give another child or two the task of creating a list of at least ten specific objects. For instance: hockey pucks, diapers, computer keyboards.

When lists are finished, suggest that somewhere in your combined lists is your new favorite dessert. You and the children will call out what's on your lists, rotating between your food prep list, the flavors list, and the objects list (in that order). For instance: "toasted mangled mango hockey pucks!" See what wacky combinations emerge, and then mix and match to get a group "favorite." But decide together that you'll never try it!

Say: **Don't try serving these goodies at your next party if you want people to come. But when God throws a party, its good stuff—forever. That's a party I want to attend!**

EXTRA-TIME ACTIVITY—OPTION 3

INQUIRING MINDS WANT TO KNOW

Time: 5 minutes
Supplies: none

Gather kids in a circle. Ask: ***What do you think it will cost you to say "yes" to Jesus? Is it worth the price? Explain.***

SESSION 12

The Story of the Mustard Seed

The Point: God helps our faith grow.
Scripture Connect: Matthew 13:31, 32

Supplies for all Session 12 activities options: pencils, prepared poster, watch with a second hand, 1 roll of paper towels, 3 Bibles, 1 bag of pretzels, jar of mustard, several glasses of water

The Basics for Leaders

This story is actually an illustration, but it's a powerful one. That mustard you glop on your hamburger doesn't start out as sauce. It's made from the seeds of a bush that can grow upwards of 10 feet tall. And that plant starts out as a seed so small that, in Jesus' day, it was the tiniest seed most of his audience had ever seen.

There's debate about what Jesus meant by "kingdom of God" in this illustration. Did he mean the number of people who would at first follow him compared with the millions to come later, or that his teaching would in time reach many more people? Either way, the point is true.

At first, thousands of people followed Jesus. But by the time he stumbled to the cross, Jesus' followers were few. And yet, one day, *everyone* will bow to him.

At one time only his disciples heard all of Jesus' teaching. Now, anyone with a Bible and the ability to read can know what he told his disciples.

No question about it: when God is there, big things come from small ones. You'll share that principle with your kids today!

OPENING ACTIVITY—OPTION 1

HOWZITGOIN'

Time: about 5 minutes, depending on attendance
Supplies: pencils, prepared poster

Before kids arrive, draw a line on a poster. Place a 1 on the left end of the line, a 10 on the right, and a 5 in the middle. As kids arrive, ask them to pencil in their initials on the line.

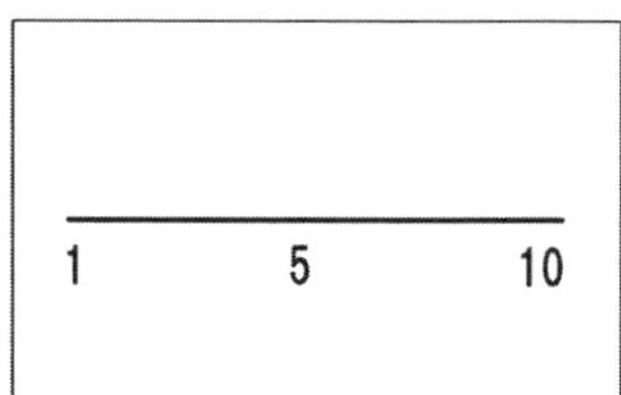

Say: **If this past week was so awful you wish you'd slept through it, place your initials by the 1. If it was a great week you wish you could repeat, put your initials by the 10. Place your initials anywhere on the line that shows how you feel about this past week—except exactly on the 5. That's because there's no such thing as a week that's exactly half good and half bad!**

After kids have signed in, give them 30 seconds each to explain why they placed their initials where they did. Be sure to include your own initials and explain your placement on the line. Kids will begin to express themselves more over time—and hearing their stories will help you adapt this lesson to make it relevant to your kids' lives.

OPENING ACTIVITY—OPTION 2

30-SECOND SERVICE

Time: about 10 minutes
Supplies: watch with a second hand

Form children into pairs. Ask children in each pair to decide who's the Mustard Seed and who will be the Tomato Seed. Give kids 10 seconds to accomplish the task, and then continue.

Say: **Mustard Seeds, in a moment you'll send your partners off to do**

a mission project. Not a week-long project in a foreign country; instead, it can take no more than 30 seconds and has to happen right here in this room.

There are three rules:

1. **The project must be helpful and positive. It's OK to send your Tomato Seed to hug me and say, "You're great!" It's not OK to send him to punch me and say, "You're ugly!"**
2. **It can't take more than 30 seconds. You can't wash all the windows in this room, but you can give someone a 20-second back rub.**
3. **If your Tomato Seed says, "I can't do that," think of something else.**

Remember, everyone, a service project isn't about what *you* want. And it may not be easy! It's all about helping someone else.

Ready? Mustard Seeds, assign projects now. (pause) **Tomato Seeds, get started right . . . *now!***

After the first round, have Mustard and Tomato Seeds change roles and play again. Then have pairs sit down, facing each other, and discuss:

- ***Which did you like more—doing the project or assigning one?***
- ***What was hard about your project? What was easy?***
- ***Your 30-second mission was a small thing—how could it have a big impact?***
- ***What's something in your life that seemed small, but turned out to be big?***

Gather kids back together and ask them to share what they learned from talking with their partners.

Say: **Today we're looking at a story Jesus told about a small thing that turned into something big. We'll see how, with God's help, that happens to our faith too!**

Cool Story Game

Towel Time

Time: 10 minutes or more

Supplies: 1 roll of paper towels

Place a length of paper towels on the floor. Allow about 18 inches of paper toweling per child. Ask children to line up on the towels facing you.

Say: **In a moment, I'll ask you to line up again on the towels, shortest person to tallest person. The catch: you can't step off the paper towels. Ready?** (You may need to step in and replace the paper towels if they become too torn.)

Have children line up shortest to tallest and then reform in these lineups:

- Youngest to oldest
- Alphabetical order of first name
- Birth dates (earliest in calendar year to latest)
- Shortest hair length to longest

If you have all younger kids, help them line up initially and then ask them to line up in easier ways, such as:

- Color of shirts (darkest to lightest)
- Ages (by years, not by birth dates)
- Eye color (lightest to darkest)

After playing, say: **Great job squirming and slithering to stay on the towels! There are lots of ways to arrange things—including us—from smallest to largest. And if we were lining up seeds from smallest to largest, down toward the smallest end would be mustard seeds. They're tiny—but if you plant them properly, something huge follows. You can get a bush that's 10 feet tall.**

Jesus used that fact in a story he told about mustard seeds. Let's dive into that story now!

Cool BIBLE STORY

MUSTARD TASTING

Time: about 15 minutes

Supplies: 3 Bibles, 1 bag of pretzels, jar of mustard, several glasses of water

Form your children into pairs for this Bible story activity. Ask pairs to sit next to each other.

Say: **Jesus' story about a mustard plant hit home with his audience in a way it doesn't hit home with us. How many of you live on farms? At least have a garden? And in your garden you have a mustard plant?**

To us, the notion of making our own mustard—of caring for the plant, harvesting the seeds, and grinding seeds to mix with other spices and vinegar or wine . . . well, all that seems strange and unknown. But to Jesus' audience, it was everyday life.

Give each child a pretzel, and then pass around the jar of mustard. Ask children to dip their pretzels in the jar and taste the mustard. (Tell kids there's no double-dipping allowed!) Have glasses of water available for children who don't like the lingering taste of mustard.

After the mustard has been sampled, collect any leftover pretzels. Say: **Strong taste! And this isn't as strong as pure mustard. The seed of a mustard plant is about the size of a pinhead. It's tiny. Yet when a mustard plant is well tended, it can grow to 10 feet or more. The people listening to Jesus knew that.**

With your partner, see if you can come up with other uses for a mustard plant. One is to provide flavor for food—but how else could people in Jesus' day have used such a big plant?

Allow time for children to share, and then ask for their suggestions. Some suggestions might include: provide shade, serve as firewood, be used as a hedge, anchor half a hammock, be a decorative plant, be used as an income source by harvesting and selling seeds, become a bird perch.

Say: **Handy things, mustard plants! And Jesus found a use none of us mentioned. Here's what he had to say.** Read aloud Matthew 13:31, 32.

Say: **Jesus used the mustard plant to teach a truth: that when God**

is involved, our faith grows. We believe, but as we feel God's love and watch God work, our faith grows strong.

That's true of how the church grew too. At first just a few people followed Jesus. Then there were a few more. But then . . . let's look up and read two passages.

Help children find these passages and read them aloud: Acts 2:41 and Acts 4:4.

Say: **The number of people coming to Jesus grew and grew. And so did their faith! God continued to multiply his followers in amazing ways—just as he multiplies our faith today!**

CLOSING PRAYER

SMALL-TO-TALL PRAYER

Time: about 5 minutes

Supplies: none

Ask children to pray with partners. Say: **Let's pray for small things that can become large, for God to take those small things and do great things with them. I'll suggest what we can pray for, and you and your partner can offer sentence prayers. For example, if I say, "Please help our family members grow by . . . " you could finish my sentence by saying, ". . . obeying you more each day." Ready?**

Pray: **God, please hear our prayers as we ask you to bless small things that you can help grow into large things.**

Please help the small children in our church grow by . . . (pause)

Please help people who are poor grow by . . . (pause)

Please help people who are scared grow by . . . (pause)

Please help us grow closer to you by . . . (pause)

And please use us in your kingdom in both large and small ways, God. Amen.

EXTRA-TIME ACTIVITY—OPTION 1

BABY FACE

Time: about 5 minutes
Supplies: none

Ask kids to sit in a circle on the floor. Say: **You started out in life small. You were a baby—and I'm sure you were all cute babies too. Let's play a game called Baby Face. There are two simple rules:**

1. **When I call out an emotion or situation, you make a baby face that matches. Keep making the face as you look at the faces of your friends here in the circle.**
2. **Do not laugh! The goal is to get other people to laugh!**

Use the list below to prompt baby faces. Add your own situations.

- You're a happy baby.
- You're a scared baby.
- You're a sleepy little baby.
- You lost your blankie.
- You're hungry.
- You're a grumpy baby.
- Uh-oh, you're about to fill your diaper!

Say: **Way to go, baby faces! I can see why your mommies thought you were cute when you were little! And even though you started out small, now you're big—kind of like mustard seeds!**

EXTRA-TIME ACTIVITY—OPTION 2

BIG. BIGGER. BIGGEST

Time: about 10 minutes
Supplies: none

Say: **For this game, it's best if you've watched a lot of nature shows on TV or you visit the zoo often. I'll call off the names of two animals. Act like the biggest of the two animals. I'll tell you if I mean biggest by**

length or by weight. For instance, if I said, "Length: snakes and giraffes," you'd lie down and stretch out. You'd imitate the longest animal! Let's try it: Length: snakes and giraffes! Ask children to be seated again. Tell them that after each animal pair they'll again be seated. Use the pairs below, and if you have older children, toss in a few of the challenge pairs.

- *Weight: moose or mosquito?*
  Moose: 1,430 pounds versus the mosquito at 2.5 milligrams
- *Length: toad or turkey?*
  Turkey: 3.75 feet versus the toad at 2.95 inches
- *Length: alligator or ant?*
  Alligator: 12.5 feet versus the ant at a half inch
- *Weight: tiger shark or tiger?*
  Tiger shark: 1,125 pounds versus the tiger at 370 pounds
- *Weight: penguin or platypus?*
  Penguin (emperor): 88 pounds versus the platypus at 3 pounds

Say: **Good job! It looked like a zoo in here!** Circle up and discuss:

- ***What's something small in your life that you'd like to see grow into something big? For instance, maybe you're playing hockey and you'd like to be a pro someday.***
- ***What does it take for that to happen?***
- ***How can you use that growing thing to serve God?***

EXTRA-TIME ACTIVITY—OPTION 3

INQUIRING MINDS WANT TO KNOW

Time: 5 minutes
Supplies: none

Gather kids in a circle. Ask: ***What will change in your life as your faith grows and becomes even bigger and stronger?***

The story of the Precious Pearl

The Point: Jesus is worth everything.
Scripture Connect: Matthew 13:45, 46

Supplies for all Session 13 activities options: pencils, prepared poster, junk drawer stuff (such as old keys, buttons, batteries), 10 rolls of toilet tissue, Bible, 1 dull and 1 shiny penny for each child (they'll keep the shiny ones), calculator, paper, watch with a second hand

The Basics for Leaders

This is a simple story—and a richer one when you have some background. In Jesus' day, pearls were far more expensive than they are today. There were no pearl farms or cultured pearls; each pearl had to be found in nature and imported.

The Romans were especially fond of pearls, and a large, perfect pearl was considered a vast treasure. The Roman historian Suetonius reported that General Vitellius financed a Roman military campaign by selling just one of his mother's pearl earrings!

So when Jesus painted the word picture of a merchant sorting among pearls and finding one that's superior—a perfect pearl—his audience understood the merchant's excitement and perhaps the merchant's willingness to give up everything to own the treasure.

Today you'll help your children discover that meaning behind Jesus' story, that there is something worth their time, devotion, possessions. That's far more valuable than anything else.

Jesus is worth everything!

OPENING ACTIVITY—OPTION 1

HOWZITGOIN'

Time: about 5 minutes, depending on attendance
Supplies: pencils, prepared poster

Before kids arrive, draw a line on a poster. Place a 1 on the left end of the line, a 10 on the right, and a 5 in the middle. As kids arrive, ask them to pencil in their initials on the line.

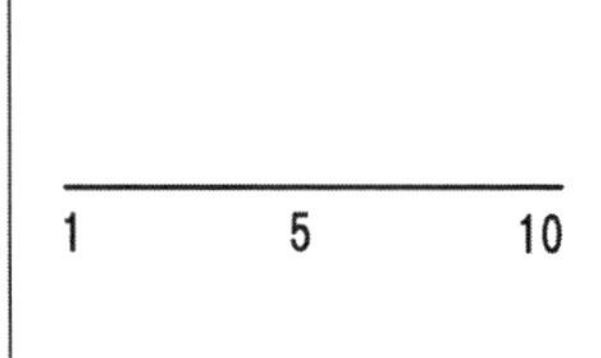

Say: **If this past week was so awful you wish you'd slept through it, place your initials by the 1. If it was a great week you wish you could repeat, put your initials by the 10. Place your initials anywhere on the line that shows how you feel about this past week—except exactly on the 5. That's because there's no such thing as a week that's exactly half good and half bad!**

After kids have signed in, give them 30 seconds each to explain why they placed their initials where they did. Be sure to include your own initials and explain your placement on the line. Kids will begin to express themselves more over time—and hearing their stories will help you adapt this lesson to make it relevant to your kids' lives.

OPENING ACTIVITY—OPTION 2

BETTER AND BETTER

Time: about 10 minutes
Supplies: junk drawer stuff (such as old keys, buttons, batteries)

Empty out the junk drawer and invite children to each take an object they especially like. Tell children they'll give the items back though!

Say: **Look carefully at the item you chose. Think about how you might use it and why it's worth more than the items you didn't take.** (pause)

After a few moments, say: **In the next three minutes, trade your item for something even better. Maybe you've got a button—hugely helpful if one pops off your shirt as you're about to give a report at school. But someone else has a battery, which you could use to power up a small transmitter to call the coast guard if your ship is about to sink. So see if you can trade your button for the battery. Try hard to make someone else trade. Go!**

After three minutes, have kids sit in a circle. Ask anyone who made a trade to explain why what he or she got was better than what was traded. Identify the item that was most traded. Ask kids to tell what their friends said to make them trade.

Collect the items and return them to the drawer. Say: **One thing that makes an item especially desirable and valuable is if the item is rare. Today we'll explore a story Jesus told about an item that was so valuable that a man went home and sold everything he owned to come up with enough money to buy it!**

Cool Story Game

Carry On

Time: 10 minutes or more

Supplies: 10 rolls of toilet tissue

Time for a trip to the discount store! You'll need at least ten rolls of toilet tissue for this game, but the rolls will be in usable shape after the game.

Place the rolls in two stacks of five rolls on one side of your room. Form your kids into two equal teams (join in if necessary to even up teams) and place one team by each stack of toilet tissue.

Say: **Let's say you're shipwrecked on a deserted island—one that has lots of fresh water, plenty of food, tons of fish waiting to be caught, and a long, beautiful beach. It's a perfect place to be stuck except for one detail: you have no toilet tissue.**

So your goal is to carry five rolls to the far wall and back again—delivering it to the needy people there on Uncomfortable Island. To carry

the rolls you must hold all five rolls across, touching only the rolls on the ends. Demonstrate how to hold and carry the rolls.

Say: **This is a relay race and time is key. Looks like some of your friends on the island are hopping around hoping you show up soon!**

After the race, discuss:

- ***What else would you miss if you were stuck on an island like I described?***
- ***What's the most expensive item you've ever bought with your own money? Why was the item worth the cost to you?***
- ***If you could sell everything you own and buy just one thing—would you do it? What would the thing be and why?***

Say: **Let's dig into a story that Jesus told about a man who gave all he had to own a pearl—one perfect pearl. Let's find out what happened.**

Cool BIBLE STORY

PENNIES AND PEARLS

Time: about 15 minutes

Supplies: Bible, 1 dull and 1 shiny penny for each child

Ask children to sit in a circle. Give each child a dull penny, but keep the shiny ones in your pocket. Say: **In a few moments I'll be telling you about a merchant who bought a pearl. Before I do, though, you need to become pearl merchants yourselves. You need to learn how to tell a regular pearl from a good pearl, and a good pearl from a great pearl. We'll practice on the pennies I've given you.**

Ask children to examine their pennies. Say: **Five things make a great pearl. Look at your pennies to see how they stack up in each category.**

Category 1 is SHAPE. In nature, very few pearls come out of an oyster round. They're lopsided. The more round a pearl, the better. Look at your

penny. Is it round? If so, you've got the start of a top-notch pearl!

Category 2 is SIZE. In pearls, the bigger, the better—if the pearl scores well in other categories. I'm assuming all your pennies are the same size, but check with your neighbor. If yours is larger than average, that's a good thing!

Category 3 is COLOR. Pearls come in many colors, with pure white being the most valued. Look at your pennies. Is your penny shiny and bright, or dull? If it's bright, your "pearl" is worth more. With pearls, the brighter, the better.

Category 4 is LUSTER. Oysters secrete calcium-carbonate crystals to cover specks of dirt or other irritants. That's what makes a pearl. If there are lots of layers of crystals and they're worn smooth, that's luster. Does your penny reflect the light well? Is it smooth, or worn out and pitted?

Category 5 is called ORIENT. If you can look at a pearl and it almost seems to glow from the inside, it has "orient." It's a matter of light refracting from the various layers. Does your penny glow? I'm guessing not—but maybe it does.

Hold up your pennies. If they were pearls, they'd be worth different amounts because of the things I've mentioned. Now imagine you made your living buying and selling pearls. You'd get very good at telling one pearl from another and knowing which one was worth the most.

Jesus' story is about a pearl merchant. He probably looked through handfuls of pearls, looking for those that would get the best price. And then, one day, he spotted this. Hold up a bright new penny. Say: **He knew he had something special. Here's what Jesus said he did.**

Read aloud Matthew 13:45, 46. Then discuss:

- ***Why do you think the merchant was eager to get the perfect pearl?***
- ***What do you think the pearl stands for in this story?***
- ***Where do we fit into the story?***

Say: **We're like the pearl merchant. We give our lives to a lot of things—but only one is perfect and that's Jesus. We can give him our old, worn-out lives and he gives us new life. New life that lasts forever!**

Ask children if they want to trade their dull, less-than-perfect pennies for the shiny ones you have. Trade, and let them keep the shiny ones.

Say: **That's what we can do with our lives: give them to Jesus and get shiny, new lives. Let's give ourselves to Jesus because Jesus is worth everything!**

CLOSING PRAYER

PERSONAL PEARL PRAYER

Time: about 5 minutes
Supplies: none

Ask children to stand in a circle, facing in, and join them. Say: **Jesus is worth everything—no question about it. But Jesus said there was something else nearly as valuable as himself. Something so important that he was willing to go through death to save it. And that's *you.***

You're a pearl of great price too, and so are the people to your left and right. Look at them and think this: The King of the Universe came and died in their place on a cross so they can be his friends. That's how important those people are and how precious they are to God. So let's silently pray for each other now. I'll start and finish—you silently fill in the middle of our prayer time.

Pray: **Dear God, thank you for your love. And for loving us so deeply that you gave your Son to rescue us. That's amazing, God, and we praise you for it.**

Hear our prayers as we pray for the people standing on our right. (pause) **And hear our prayers as we pray for the people standing on our left.** (pause) **You're so good, God. We love you. Amen.**

EXTRA-TIME ACTIVITY—OPTION 1

PEARL PRICING

Time: about 10 minutes
Supplies: calculator, 1 sheet of paper and 1 pencil per child

This activity is best suited for older kids who are good at multiplying very large numbers! You may wish to do this activity together using a calculator instead of old-fashioned multiplication.

Give each child a sheet of paper and a pencil. Say: **The largest—and most expensive—pearl is the Pearl of Lao Tzu. (Good luck pronouncing that!) It weighs 14.1 pounds and is valued at nearly $60 million. Let's round that off to 14 pounds at $60 million . . . or $4,285,714.29 per pound. We'll round that off to $4,286,000 per pound—write that down.** Help younger children write the amount.

Here's my question: using pearl pricing, what are you worth? Multiply your weight in pounds by $4,286,000, and let's see what you're worth. You don't have to share the total—but do take a look at that number! If you get stuck, I've got a calculator to use, and I'll help.

After numbers are totaled, as a group discuss:

- ***What would you do with that much money?***
- ***What can Jesus do for you that the Pearl of Lao Tzu can't do?***

EXTRA-TIME ACTIVITY—OPTION 2

PRICE TAGS

Time: about 5 minutes

Supplies: 1 sheet of paper and 1 pencil per child, watch with a second hand

Ask children to tear their paper into ten or twelve pieces. Say: **In a few moments I'll ask you to quickly put a price tag on everything in this room. Write down what you think the item is worth and place the tag on or near the item. Then move along to the next item, because you've got to go through all your price tags in just 72 seconds! If there's already a price tag on an item, find something that hasn't yet been priced.** (If you have younger kids, consider pairing them with older kids as they price their items.)

Start the timer and set kids free. When 72 seconds have gone by, have kids sit down in a circle. Collect pencils and extra price tags. Walk around the room and announce some of the estimates, asking whoever wrote the amount to defend his or her estimate. Have fun with this!

Come back to the circle and say: **I'm not sure what anything in this room is worth except for a very few items. And those I can price exactly.**

Walk around the circle touching each child's shoulder in turn and addressing the child by name, such as, "Frank, you are priceless." Explain that *priceless* means they're so valuable, there's no number big enough to use for their price tags.

Say: **How can I know you're worth so much? Because Jesus is beyond price, and he chose to come to earth and die on the cross in your place. He finds you so valuable that he was willing to go through death for you. That's how much you're worth. That's how much God loves you.**

EXTRA-TIME ACTIVITY—OPTION 3

INQUIRING MINDS WANT TO KNOW

Time: 5 minutes
Supplies: none

Gather kids in a circle. Ask: ***Jesus is worth everything. He's a pearl beyond price. Great—but how does that change how you'll live tomorrow?***

About the Author

Mikal Keefer has published more than twenty books and is a frequent contributor to Group Publishing curriculum. He wrote Group's *Heroes Unmasked,* a fall festival program that was the recipient of the 2006 Outstanding Children's Ministry Resource Award from *Outreach* magazine. He's an active volunteer leader in children's ministry at Church of the Good Shepherd in Loveland, Colorado. Mikal is married and the father of two children. For years he and his wife were not involved in a small group because they didn't know what to do with the kids! That's why he is so passionate about offering this solution.